THE WHOLE OF LIFE
for CHRIST

THE WHOLE OF LIFE for CHRIST

The Keswick Year Book 2015

Liam Goligher
Paul Mallard
John Risbridger
Mark Greene
Tim Chester
Vanessa Conant
Malcolm Duncan
Robin Sydserff
Patrick Fung
Martin Salter
George Verwer

First published 2016

British Library Cataloguing in Publication Data
A catalogue record for this book is available from the British Library.

ISBN: 978–1–78359–408–5

Set in Dante 12.5/16pt
Typeset in Great Britain by CRB Associates, Potterhanworth, Lincolnshire
Printed and bound in Great Britain by Ashford Colour Press Ltd, Gosport, Hampshire

Contents

The Addresses

Introduction

The comedian Spike Milligan was once taking a train journey when someone asked him where he came from. 'From London,' he said. So his fellow traveller replied, 'Which part?' To which Spike Milligan replied, 'All of me'.

It's a good answer! At Keswick 2015 the theme was: 'The Whole of Life for Christ'. We know that God is not interested simply in my verbal profession of faith or my occasional religious activity. He wants all of me. He wants every aspect of my life to reflect his glory and fulfil his purpose. He wants us to serve Christ in every arena of life, not simply in the Christian environments of church and home, but in our work, in our communities, in our politics, in our recreation and in every sphere of life to which he calls us.

The following chapters provide a great sample of the teaching given at the 2015 Convention, with a variety of speakers ranging across different parts of the Bible, but all with a desire to be faithful to Scripture and contemporary in application. The 2015 event attracted over 12,000 people of all ages, and there was a warm response to the teaching, including the wide range of seminars, the morning Bible expositions and the evening celebrations. Many came to faith in Christ, many committed their lives to the cause of global mission and many gave their lives more fully to Christ and his service, wherever he might call them. We praise God for all of these positive results of the Word at work, in the power of the Spirit.

Alongside this Year Book, we would like to recommend that you also use the Keswick Study Guide for 2015, *The Whole of Life for Christ: Enriching Everyday Discipleship*, written by Antony Billington and Mark Greene, and published for Keswick by IVP. This is how the Study Guide is described on its back cover:

> Suppose for a moment that Jesus really is interested in every aspect of your life. Everything – the dishes and the dog and the day job and the drudgery of some of the stuff you just have to do, the TV programme you love, the staff in your local supermarket as well as the homeless in the local shelter, your boss as well as your vicar, helping a shopper find the ketchup as well as brewing the tea for the life group, the well-being of your town and the well-being of your neighbour . . .
>
> Suppose the truth that every Christian is a new creature in Christ, empowered by the Spirit to do his will, means

that Christ is with you everywhere you go, in every task you do, with every person you meet . . .

Suppose God wants to involve you in what he's doing in the places you spend your time day by day . . .

Suppose your whole life is important to Christ . . .

It is.

These seven studies will help you explore and live out the marvellous truth that the gospel is an invitation into whole-life discipleship, into a life following and imitating Jesus.

You can order the Study Guide through www.ivpbooks. com.

And at the end of this Year Book you will also find a note about all the mp3s, CDs and DVDs which record every aspect of the 2015 Convention programme, across all three weeks. This represents a fantastic resource, and we would like to encourage you to download free mp3s from our website: https://keswickministries.org/resources/ keswick-talk-downloads. Or to order the great products from the 2015 Convention provided by Essential Christian, go to: www.essentialchristian.com/keswick. Please do spread the word!

At the final meeting of the Convention, I mentioned to the congregation how many good things had happened.

Over 12,000 people have been with us, some 2,000 children and young people, with 39 teaching events at the main tent, 65 seminars, 70 children's events, 88 youth gigs,

30 for 19–24s, 31 church services, 37 other meetings of various kinds.

Then 15,000 teaching sessions have been sold by Essential Christian on DVD, CD and USB sticks in the past three weeks, all around the world; over 26,000 books have been sold by ThinkIVP in three weeks; on Clayton Television there have been 10,000 plays each week of this year's Bible readings; we've had 8,500 mp3 downloads of messages from our website.

There have been hundreds of songs sung, thousands of prayers prayed, several thousand people have followed us on Facebook, Twitter and live-streaming to YouTube, 1.5 million people listened to Keswick on Radio 4, and several million will watch BBC TV *Songs of Praise* from Keswick this year. Praise the Lord!

But what really matters – the measure of how effective these weeks have been – will be seen in changed lives, lives that are wholeheartedly committed to Jesus Christ and his cause. What really counts is reflected in our strapline – that, *having heard God's Word, we become like God's Son and we serve God's mission.*

We pray the same for every reader of this book!

Jonathan Lamb
CEO and minister-at-large, Keswick Ministries

The Bible Readings

Radical Kingdom

by Liam Goligher

Liam Goligher is a native of Scotland and pastored churches in Ireland, Canada, Scotland and England before moving to Tenth Presbyterian Church, Philadelphia in 2011. He has long been associated with university ministry and has been deeply involved with Keswick ministry for many years. Liam is married to Christine and they have five children, seven grandchildren and a dog Chloe.

Radical Kingdom: Matthew 5:1–16

As we come to Matthew chapter 5, one of the questions you might be asking yourself is: 'What can Liam say that's new?' Well, very little. But one of the things we need to do before we even begin to look at this passage is to see the way in which Matthew considers this sermon crucial evidence for his fundamental thesis that Jesus Christ is the divine King, the divine Son of God, the Messiah that was long expected.

Throughout Matthew's Gospel you will find explicit references to the Old Testament. In the first couple of pages of Matthew's Gospel quotations from the Old Testament stand out. There are other ones that don't stand out; they are merely lines that are quoted. You will also find Jesus using words like 'poor', 'mourn', 'meek', 'righteousness' and 'pure', which are loaded with Old Testament meaning.

One of the things you will discover as you read the New Testament is the way in which these writers understand the Old Testament, especially the Psalms, and prophets like Isaiah.

Jesus too is very conscious that he is acting out his life according to a script that was written by the Spirit and, as you see various times in the Old Testament, agreed upon by the Father and the Son. They planned this great drama of redemption, with Jesus as the lead actor in the story. And it's hard to escape the influence of the Old Testament, as you look at the events that unfold leading up to chapter 5. We can't listen to Matthew's sermon without seeing what he has already said about Jesus.

Whereas Luke's Gospel begins with the beginning, the Son of God, and then Adam and so on, Matthew is very concerned to show Jesus as the Messiah and the one who is fulfilling the promises that God made to Israel. And so, he begins with a great long genealogy which places Jesus right in the flow of biblical history, from Abraham, through David, down to his parents.

When the Holy Spirit inspires the angel to speak to Joseph, we learn that this one who will come is Immanuel, God with us. As Isaiah prophesied, 'The virgin will conceive and give birth to a son, and will call him Immanuel' (Isaiah 7:14). Then, throughout his book, Isaiah develops this theme that the one who is coming is in fact God. So, by the time you reach Isaiah 40, he is describing someone who will come in preparation for the arrival of God. And in Matthew 3:3, we find Isaiah 40 quoted as John the Baptist is introduced to us, as the voice who prepares the way of the Lord. This one who is coming is God with us – he is the Lord whom Isaiah anticipated would come to bring the reign of God, the rule of God, the kingdom of God, to bear upon the earth.

Jesus, in chapter 2 of Matthew, is described as 'Israel'. He is the son who is taken down into Egypt for safety and brought back to the Promised Land. We have overtures of Isaiah 49, where God identifies his servant who will restore Israel to himself. God's servant would redeem Israel and bring them back to the land that he had given to them.

At Jesus' baptism the Father quotes from Psalm 2:7:

You are my son;
    today I have become your father.

In other words, at the time of David the Son already existed. In the very midst of antiquity and eternity, the Son was begotten by the Father, and the Father says to his Son, 'This is my Son, whom I love; with him I am well pleased' (Matthew 3:17). Jesus, the one who is arriving on the scene, is the eternal, divine Son of the Father, sharing the very nature of God, according to Psalm 2.

Next Matthew brings us to the temptation. Jesus' position, both as the Saviour of Israel and as the Son of God, is put at risk, as there in the desert he recapitulates the story of Israel and is tempted by the evil one. His authority is challenged, but, like a mighty warrior, he crushes Satan by the Word of God. And then he sweeps off to Galilee, fulfilling the great prophesies of Isaiah that his ministry would begin there (Isaiah 9). And with his coming, light dawns upon the earth. He comes to the Gentiles in the land of Naphtali, and there he begins to preach (Matthew 4:15–17).

If you know your Bible, you are already thinking of places like Isaiah 40 and 52, where the one comes preaching good news. Also Isaiah 61:1–2:

> . . . the LORD has anointed me
> to proclaim good news to the poor . . .
> to comfort all who mourn.

You begin to realize that in the book of Isaiah you have the script for the action that is now about to take place, as Jesus, who is the eternal Son of God, preaches the good news and brings the kingdom of God. Here is Jesus, the faithful and true Israel, who begins to demonstrate his power over evil by crushing Satan, as Isaiah had predicted. He goes on to heal, and exorcize evil spirits, as tangible signs that the day of deliverance, the day of salvation, has arrived.

Huge numbers follow him, and Jesus selects from the crowd his own disciples. It is his disciples who now gather around him on the mountain. You need to understand that in the New Testament every word has been chosen and placed there by the Holy Spirit. So when you read that this is happening on a mountain, you think to yourself, Daniel chapter 2, where the kingdom of God comes like a little stone that will roll down the hill and across the plain, gathering momentum to become a great mountain – the kingdom of God. Or you think of Isaiah chapter 2, where in the last days the mountain of the house of the Lord will rise above all the other mountains. The Word of God will go forth from Jerusalem, and people will come to the mountain and hear the Word of God. They will come to the knowledge of God, be led in the paths of righteousness and obedience, as they come under the influence of the Word of God.

Suddenly you realize that when Jesus goes up that mountain, he is recapitulating the expectations of Judaism; he is recapitulating the script that was written for him by the Holy Spirit and communicated through the mouth of Isaiah and the mouth of David. Jesus is fulfilling the very plans of the ages as he now gathers believers around him, the remnant of Israel. There on that mountain he stakes his claim to be the final temple of God, the final resting place of the presence of God. He is there amongst his people as the light of the world, as the glory of Israel. And there, as he gathers his people, have in your mind the great gatherings you read about in the Pentateuch as Moses gathered the people of God around Mount Sinai and God came down and spoke. For as we listen to Jesus speaking in this sermon, we are not listening to Moses, who heard the Word of God from God's lips; we are listening to God himself speaking to his people.

Now, as we come to the sermon, we ask ourselves, 'What is the main point? What is the thesis text of Jesus' sermon?'

And we have to say that the thesis text of this sermon is in Matthew 5:17–18:

> Do not think that I have come to abolish the Law or the Prophets; I have not come to abolish them but to fulfil them. For truly I tell you, until heaven and earth disappear, not the smallest letter, not the least stroke of a pen, will by any means disappear from the Law until everything is accomplished.

This statement of Jesus has had a profound effect on Jewish scholarship. The renowned Jewish Scholar Jacob Neusner, in an interview about his book *A Rabbi Talks with Jesus*,[1] said that he found Jesus' approach to the Law something that was disturbing and unsettling for him. It made him want to go to Jesus and ask him the question: 'Who do you think you are? God?' What we are going to find as we read through this sermon is that Jesus is speaking to his new Israel, assembled before him in a kind of covenant renewal ceremony. As he speaks to them, it is a fresh word from heaven that does not contradict what was said before, but sharpens it, focuses it, and sets the tenor for what is to come in the entire book of Matthew.

The inheritance of Jesus' people

Let's look at the inheritance of Jesus' people. He opened his mouth and he taught them saying, 'Blessed are the poor in spirit.' It is very easy for us to take that word 'poor' and look at it economically and sociologically. But in the Bible, and certainly in the Old Testament, which is being quoted by Jesus here, the word 'poor' has to do with the remnant within Israel who were true believers. Israel was all over the place spiritually. They received the Word of God, they received the Ten Commandments and they were told to worship the Lord God only, but they worshipped God in heaven and the idols of the nations round about. They never gave their whole hearts to the worship of the God of Israel. And because of that, they lost their land and were scattered: the top ten tribes of the north disappeared, merging with the nations round about, and lost their identity; the southern kingdom of Judah was exiled into Babylon. And even after the exile, although a few came back, they were never really restored to their land; they never really knew an identity as a separate nation under God ever again. They were always under the throne of the Persians, the Greeks and then the Romans by the time Jesus comes.

When Jesus arrives, he is looking for the remnant. So, he speaks to the poor in spirit, the humble poor, who, no matter what their physical or material needs, were nonetheless humble and contrite in heart. They understood that they were impoverished before God; they understood that they were entirely dependent on God; they cast themselves on God – they had nowhere else to go. That's what it means to be spiritually poor. To be spiritually poor means to know that I have nothing in myself that I can barter with, bargain with or engage with in any kind of deal with

God. I am completely dependent on the grace of God and I realize that my utter need is for God to save me. Isaiah 61 says the humble poor have the good news preached to them.

And these people, this remnant of people, are broken-hearted people; they are those who mourn. The Messiah is said in Isaiah 61:1–2, 'to bind up the broken-hearted . . . comfort all who mourn'. Why are they grieving? Why do they need comforting by God? Isaiah 40 tells us that the comfort of God comes to those who recognize that they are sinners, who mourn over their sin. Their hearts are broken because they have rebelled against God, and they know that they deserve God's displeasure. And there in Isaiah 40 we are told that the comfort that comes to them is this: their warfare is ended, their battle with God has come to an end and their iniquity is pardoned. These are the people Jesus calls to himself – believers, trusters, those who abandon themselves to him, who mourn over their sin, who are humble and meek. They are not people who are full of themselves, swaggering around in their arrogance; they are meek because they know that they are nothing apart from God's grace in their lives.

And then there are those who hunger and thirst for righteousness. Throughout the book of Isaiah you find this theme of righteousness. When the Messiah comes, what is he going to do? Well, he is going to establish his people like oaks of righteousness, a planting of the Lord that he might be glorified. The one who comes is the servant of the

Lord. Isaiah 53 says he is 'the righteous servant' (verse 11) who lays down his life in order that he might make other people righteous. And the righteousness that God works in our lives comes in two parts. First of all, it is a righteous standing with God, when I am declared to be right with God. Once I was under condemnation, but now I am righteous in the eyes of God – that is what the word 'justify' means. God declares me righteous because of what Jesus has done for me – both by his perfect life, credited to my account, and by his death, paying the price of my rebellion and sin, being credited to my account so that by his life and by his death, by his obedience and his blood, I am declared right with God.

But be sure of this: the God who declares us righteous then sets about the task of making us righteous, making us want to be right with him in the decisions we make, in the way we think, in the things we do. This is the characteristic of Jesus' people: they hunger and thirst for righteousness. Here Jesus is telling us what they hunger and thirst for. They don't hunger and thirst for fame, health, wealth and happiness in this life. They hunger and thirst, first of all, to know that they are right with God, and second, that they might appear righteous before God. That's what they crave, that's why they come to Keswick, that's why they read Bible books, that's why they are interested in their Bible studies and why they go to church, among other things – so that God might continue his work in their lives and they would become more and more like Jesus.

People who long to be righteous realize they are not righteous; they have broken God's Law and deserve his displeasure. Nonetheless, in God's mercy they have been pardoned. And when you have been pardoned yourself, it should, over time, make you gentler with people who sin against you. I mean, we have sinned against almighty God. We deserve the displeasure of almighty God, the maker and shaker of heaven and earth. When somebody sins against me, I understand that that is a far less serious thing in cosmic terms. When I have known the mercy of God towards me, then I am merciful to other people.

And then, not only are they merciful, but they are pure in heart. Jesus takes this idea of being pure in heart straight out of Psalm 24. If you are familiar with Psalm 24, you will know that it has three parts. Part one tells us that God is already on his holy hill. He is already at Mount Zion, the temple mount in Jerusalem. That is God's earthly address where he was pleased to meet with his people. There in the temple was the Ark of the Covenant. Inside it had a rod, the Ten Commandments and some of the manna from which they used to make the manna bread when they were out in the desert. The top of the Ark of the Covenant was covered in gold. There were two gold cherubim, and in the middle was the mercy seat, which was God's throne, his earthly throne, as it were. And so, in that first part of Psalm 24, we are told that God is already at his earthly address, waiting for his people to come to him.

Then the question is asked by the Holy Spirit, 'Who may ascend the mountain of the LORD?' (verse 3). And who can stand in this holy place? Who can go right up there into the temple of God into the presence of God and not be consumed?' The answer: 'The one who has clean hands and a pure heart'. Jesus says that the pure in heart will see God. The pure of heart will not just get to God's earthly address in Jerusalem; the pure in heart will get into the heavenly presence of God. And in the heavenly presence of God, it is their destiny one day to look upon him and to see God in Christ in all his splendour and all his glory. And you say, 'How can that be? How can I, with the impurities of my life? Even though I aspire to have pure hands and a clean heart, how can I possibly get there?' And the third part of that psalm gives the answer. Another figure comes on the scene and asks, 'Who is this?' It is the Lord of hosts. It's the Lord mighty in battle. Where is he going? He's going to ascend the hill of the Lord; he is going to dwell in the holy place where the Lord is. What is his name? His name is 'the LORD'.

Psalm 24 is one of those conundrums, isn't it? We read of the existence of the Lord. Who is the Lord? The Lord is Yahweh, the covenant God of Israel. Who is the one who is approaching the Lord? He is also Yahweh; he is also the covenant God of Israel. But he comes from the desert, from Israel, and he comes towards Jerusalem, his holy city, just as he would on Palm Sunday, on that little horse, through the gates, into the city to receive the welcome of God's people. This is Jesus. And he comes fresh from the battle, just as Jesus does here in Matthew 5. He has come fresh from the battle with Satan in the desert; he has come fresh from battle with demons and disease all over

Galilee of the nations. And he's come to this mountain, he's gathered his people around him and he is saying to them,

> Blessed are the pure in heart,
>   for they will see God.

It's these people who then proclaim the good news of peace to others. The Messiah himself preaches peace to the nations. He comes proclaiming good news of peace to those who are at war with God. And his people are peacemakers: they share the good news of peace, and proclaim peace and reconciliation to others in the world. They tell people the good news that they too can be at peace with God. And the peacemakers are blessed. And they are persecuted.

Now, if you put all of these things together, you have a picture of Jesus' people. This is a kind of composite picture of what a believer looks like. This is where we are going, this is what we are about and this is what God wants to do in our lives. That is why we are at Keswick – we want the Word of God to reproduce in our lives that kind of profile, that we might be that kind of people.

And this is where Jesus, as the great Teacher, comes in. He says, in the first and last beatitudes that bracket this whole section, 'Theirs is the kingdom of heaven.' That's where God reigns, where God is in control over his people. As the Messiah proclaims the latter-day blessings over the people, he says that they belong to the kingdom of heaven. Why the kingdom of heaven? Matthew is writing to the

Jews, and the Jews didn't like to say the name 'God'. They used a euphemism. They referred to God's dwelling place rather than to God himself, but they meant the same thing. And you will notice in the Gospels that the kingdom of God and the kingdom of heaven are interchangeable expressions. And what Jesus is saying is that the kingdom of heaven belongs to people who know where they stand before God: who are poor in spirit; who grieve over their sins; who are humble because they know their position in the world; who hunger and thirst to be righteous; who proclaim the good news of peace to others, as they have the opportunity, and are persecuted for it.

Israel had lost its land by the time of Jesus, but he says to his new Israel, 'You will inherit the land.' The land is not a bit of real estate in Palestine; the land is the whole earth, the planet, this universe transformed. Paul says that the whole earth, right now, is caught up in this bondage to despair, as it realizes it is decaying. It is longing for the day of the revelation of the sons of God, because on that day even the earth will be renewed, transformed. The earth will be redeemed when Jesus returns and brings everything under the authority of his Father. He will transform the world, and the decay that we see all around us will be eradicated once and for all. That is the inheritance of Jesus' people.

The experience of Jesus' people

What is the experience of Jesus' people? He goes on to underline that, doesn't he? In chapter 5, verse 11, having

completed the beatitudes in verse 10, he adds another one
here which fills out the previous one. He says,

> Blessed are you when people insult you, persecute you
> and falsely say all kinds of evil against you because of
> me. Rejoice and be glad, because great is your reward in
> heaven, for in the same way they persecuted the prophets
> who were before you.

There is opposition to Jesus' people; there is rejection for
Jesus' people – these beatitudes belong together. Opposition and resistance to Jesus' church is an inevitable part of
being a church in the world. And Jesus says that when we
are persecuted, we stand alongside the prophets who were
faithful to the Word of God. In verse 12 Jesus draws this
direct line from the prophets to his church. It is our faithfulness to his Word that leads to the persecution of the
church.

As long as we are prepared to surrender chunks of the
Bible, the world will not assault us. But as soon as we resist,
the world sees the kingdom of God as a threat. Well, of
course it's a threat! The kingdom of God challenges every
value of the world's system. It confronts the thoughts,
attitudes, values and agendas of a world that is in rebellion
against King Jesus. And those of us who are committed to
the crown rights of our Redeemer – the one who reigns
over us as the mediator, King and head of his church – will
inevitably face resistance. That is the experience of the
church; that is the script for God's people.

The influence for Jesus' people

In these verses we see the inheritance of Jesus' people, the experience of Jesus' people and, thirdly, in verse 13 and following, the influence for Jesus' people in the world. That's almost a contradiction. We've said on the one hand that there is going to be a resistance to Jesus' people, and yet at the same time there will be an influence for Jesus' people. How is that going to be achieved? Well, the influence is both negative and positive. We are to be the salt of the earth and the light of the world. Salt was used in the ancient world to bring flavour, as well as to act as a preservative. You rubbed salt into the meat in order to preserve it; there wasn't refrigeration in those days, and salt, especially in Palestine, was ubiquitous. Why does the world need to be preserved? The world needs to be preserved because the world's system is inherently rotten, polluted and foul. The world is fallen, sinful and evil. Left to itself, the world will fester, and germs of evil in the very body of humanity will increase. But how are we to be salt in the world? We don't act as salt in the world by forgetting our saltiness. We don't preserve the world by caving in to the world. We don't add flavour by becoming like the world. Jesus says you will preserve the world, you will act as a restraint upon wickedness, just by being there. He's not talking about a movement or a special project. He's just talking about his people being the way he's described them in those beatitudes.

A little while ago, I read this piece by Professor Michael Kruger, who reminds us that in the second century, as

Christianity emerged with a distinctive religious identity, the pagan culture wasn't pleased to see it, because Christians looked different from everything else they knew. They were different because they would not pay homage to the multiple gods, and they had a distinct sexual ethic. In the first century when Christianity came into the world, Romans had multiple sexual partners, homosexual encounters, engagements with temple prostitutes, sexual affairs between mothers and sons, father and daughters, brothers and sisters, or experimentation between animals, and sharing round of wives. The Roman world was far more highly sexed than ours, so what we are experiencing today is not new to the church. But it is a reminder, Kruger goes on to say, of why Christianity survived. Christianity survived because it did not go along with the ever-changing sexual norms of the world, because to do so is a violation of the clear teachings of Scripture. It not only robs us of our great witnessing opportunities, but, for example, our defence of biblical marriage, which is built into the warp and woof of how God has made us in his image. Marriage reflects Christ's love for the church, and our commitment to marriage is a means of proclaiming the love of Jesus to the world. We are the salt of the earth, and you don't make a difference by becoming like the world.

It is very interesting that, as soon as the Supreme Court made a decision to legalize or redefine marriage, some of the mega churches in America discovered that they could make the Bible say it was all right to go along with that. That was not a principle decision; they were merely going along with the flow of the current culture: they are not the salt of the earth and they are not the light of the world. In Isaiah 49:6 the Messiah who comes to regather Israel and bring them back to God is the light of the earth. And now here is the light of the world. Jesus is saying to his people, 'You are the light of the world, by your connection to me you are the light of the world – you have the light that transforms people, that brings them to God. Only you know where to point when men and women are looking for purpose and reason. Only you know the way of salvation for people in the world. Only you have at your fingertips, in your mind, in your heart and on your lips the one name under heaven by which they must be saved, only you. Only you can bring light to the nations.'

This isn't a campaign, by the way; neither of these statements is an imperative. Jesus is not saying, 'Be the salt' and 'Be the light.' He is saying, 'You are salt and you are light, by virtue of who you are and what you are. By virtue of the fact that you are gathered to God through Jesus.' The fact that there is a church in the world is a light to the world; it condemns the world as well as inviting the world back to God. The very presence of the church is a standing statement to the world of the reality of God.

So let me just recap in a few seconds. Jesus comes onto the scene as God with us, the eternal son of God, the new, perfect, true and faithful Israel embodied in his own person: 'I am the true vine.' He begins to collect to himself, not just the branches that were attached genetically and relationally to him as the true Israel, but branches that bring forth fruit to his glory. Those branches are his church, his people; they are you and I. We come this morning with a heart for God, a cry in our innermost beings that God would be real to us, that he would come amongst us and do something in our lives. May God answer that heart cry. May God use his Word to reproduce in us the kind of good works by which the world will glorify God.

Note

1. Jacob Neusner, *A Rabbi Talks with Jesus* (McGill-Queen's University Press, 2000).

The Mystery of Providence

by Paul Mallard

Since he was called to pastoral ministry in 1982, Paul has served as pastor of churches in Chippenham and Worcester. For four years he was part of a pastoral team in a church in Birmingham, while being engaged in itinerant ministry throughout the UK. He has recently become the pastor of Widcombe Baptist Church in Bath. Paul is married to Edrie and they have four children and five grandchildren. He is a lifetime supporter of West Bromwich Albion.

The Mystery of Providence:
2 Kings 4:8–37

The whole of the Bible, everything from beginning to end, is about Jesus. There is one hero, one story, one person it is all focused on – Jesus. In the New Testament Jesus is present, proclaimed, preached and, in Revelation, pre-eminent. But what about the Old Testament? Well, in the Old Testament Jesus is predicted, prophesied and pre-figured. For example, he's spoken of clearly in the prophecy of Psalm 22 and Isaiah 53. And then there is a particular way that the Old Testament draws our attention to Jesus, and this is known as 'typology' or 'types'. A type is a real object, event, person or place, which was divinely ordained by God to be a prophetic picture or shadow of the good things that he would bring about in Jesus Christ.

So, for example, the sacrificial system in Leviticus 1 – 7 is a shadow and a picture of Jesus. You take a lamb and make a sacrifice for your sin, but that is only a picture or a token; Jesus is the Lamb of God who takes away the sin of the world. Prophets, priests or kings are shadows and pictures of Jesus. And Elisha is a type of Christ.

Look at the parallels – their names are similar: Yeshua (Jesus) means 'Yahweh, the Lord, saves'; Elisha means 'God saves'. Both begin their ministry at the River Jordan. Both come out of the Jordan in the power of the Spirit. Both have a ministry that is dominated by grace. Both fed the hungry, healed lepers, raised the dead, and at the end of their lives life came from their tombs.

But there is one thing we need to add to this. The thing that the type is pointing to is known as the antitype, and the antitype is always greater than the type. If you look at Elisha, he is only a dim reflection of Jesus. When Jesus comes, you get the reality. So, compare the miracles of Elisha with those of Jesus: 100 men fed; 5,000/6,000 fed. Elisha heals one leper, but Jesus heals ten lepers! An axe head floats; Jesus walks on water. Elijah prays for life, but Jesus is the Lord of life. Look at the shadow, and then turn your eyes to the reality.

If you have your Bible, please turn to 2 Kings 4:8–37. It's a three-act play. In verses 8–17 a son is given; in verses 18–28 a son is taken and in verses 29–37 a son is returned. It's a very honest and realistic passage about childlessness, the wonderful gift of a child and then the child's death. It was tough in those days. But it's tough today. Christians get cancer and Alzheimer's. We suffer broken homes, broken relationships, broken marriages, and we have kids who break our hearts. And into that situation, the only comfort and hope I can give is to turn our eyes to the Lord: to gaze at him and learn something about him.

That's what we are going to do today. We are going to see three things about the Lord from this passage. First of all, we are going to see that God's generosity is incredible; secondly, that God's plans are inscrutable; and thirdly, that God's power is invincible.

God's generosity is incredible

Number one: God's generosity is incredible. Look at verse 8: 'One day Elisha went to Shunem.' Now, Shunem was a little village, just south of the Sea of Galilee, on a hill called Moreh. Elisha has an itinerant ministry, and day after day this woman watches him walking along the road. She is a very generous woman, 'well-to-do' – the word literally means 'a great woman'. She sees Elisha and suddenly she has this brilliant idea. She says, 'Come and have a meal!' So, whenever he came past, she opened her house and gave him a meal. And then she wanted to go a little bit further. Look at verse 9: 'She said to her husband, "I know that this man who often comes our way is a holy man of God."' She's great in wealth, and she's also great in spiritual insight. She sees this is the man of God, with the Word of God.

She wants to bless this man, so she feeds him. But more than that, she sets up this little room, and every time Elisha comes, that's his bolthole – it's a place to escape to. This woman is incredibly generous. She is a personification of Lady Wisdom – she loves the Lord, she fears the Lord, she's got physical resources and she wants to be generous with them. It's wonderful to meet generous Christians, isn't it? The good news, as far as the Derwent Project is concerned, is that all the money is available. The bad news is that it is still in your pockets! Generosity is wonderful, but the sad thing is that we don't often see it. And actually, as disciples, there's one thing we can all do. Whether we've got lots or little, we can use our home as an outpost for the kingdom of God, as a place where people can come and be blessed.

Next, this generous woman meets a generous God. In verse 12 we read that Elisha has been resting and,

> He said to his servant Gehazi, 'Call the Shunammite.' So he called her, and she stood before him. Elisha said to him, 'Tell her, "You have gone to all this trouble for us. Now what can be done for you? Can we speak on your behalf to the king or the commander of the army?"'

At this point Elisha is in a fairly significant position – he has the ear of the king. I think the woman's response is absolutely stunning. Look at verse 13: she replied, 'I have a home among my own people.' Basically, she is saying, 'I've got everything I need. I don't need anything.' She's satisfied. She's got all that she needs in her home, but she's also got the man of God, with the Word of God – isn't that fantastic?

Many years ago a dear woman in our church, who had been a missionary, lived in a Christian retirement home.

When she died, she had just about enough money to pay for a pauper's funeral. But the church said, she's not going to have a pauper's funeral; we are going to put on a good do for her because she was such a wonderful servant of God. She only possessed a well-read Bible, three books and one change of clothing. That was all she had in the world. Everything else she had given away. I'll never forget her funeral. Someone who had worked with her on the mission field stood up and said, 'She left nothing at all as far as this world's goods are concerned, but she didn't worry about that, because she was totally satisfied with Jesus.' Totally satisfied with Jesus. Wouldn't you like someone to say that at your funeral? That's what this woman says.

In verse 14 Elisha says to Gehazi, 'What can be done for her?'

Gehazi says, 'She has no son, and her husband is old.'

In those days there was a particular tragedy in having no children. It was also a theological tragedy, because the hope was that the one who would come and crush the serpent's head would come through a male child. So there is a secret need in her life. And what does Elisha do? He asks Gehazi to call her and then tells her, 'About this time next year you will hold a son in your arms' (verse 16). The phrase is very interesting: 'At the time of living you will hold a son in your arms.' Literally, it means, 'In the springtime, when life comes back, you will hold a child.' The same phrase is used in Genesis 18 when God tells Sarah that at 'this time next year, you will have a child'. This promise seems too good to be true. 'That's impossible,' she says. But the Lord answers the prophet's word, and 'the woman became pregnant and the next year about that same time she gave birth to a son, just as Elisha had told her' (verse 17).

Dale Ralph Davis explains that there are seven occasions in the Bible where you get a miraculous baby.[1] The first one is Isaac: the promise had to go through Isaac to bring about the purposes of God. Jacob and Joseph are miraculous babies. Joseph needed to be born in order to protect the people of God, as did Samson. Samuel was a miraculous baby, and he was needed in order to bring back the kingship. And, of course, in the New Testament, the one that trumps them all is John the Baptist. John the Baptist is born in a supernatural way in order to point forward to Jesus, whose birth transcends all of them! All these babies, although born in a natural way, through a father and a mother, are born supernaturally, because the father or mother was too old, whereas with Jesus it is a miracle of another order. Jesus is born of a virgin, and so the Word becomes flesh.

What about this boy? What was his name? What was the name of his mum? What did his dad do? We don't know. What was the great impact that this boy made for the kingdom of God? None really, as far as we can tell. Why did God give this child to this woman? Well, the answer is, it was just the generosity of God's heart. Here was a woman in need, and in his wonderful generosity God wanted to bless her. That's Dale Ralph Davis's point, and I think it's true! The Lord is amazingly generous. And, as Christians, we need to grasp that, because very often we don't think of God in quite those terms. Think of Psalm 103:

Bless the LORD O my soul,
and all that is within me,
bless his holy name!
Bless the LORD, O my soul,
and forget not all his benefits,
who forgives all your iniquity,
who heals all your diseases,
who redeems your life from the pit . . .
The LORD is . . . slow to anger and abounding
in steadfast love . . .
He does not deal with us according to our sins . . .
as far as the east is from the west,
so far does he remove our transgressions from us.
As a father shows compassion to his children,
so the LORD shows compassion to those who fear him.
(verses 1–13 ESV)

Often Christians think of God as rather mean and short-tempered. He's just waiting for us to step out of line, and then 'zap' – he's going to get us! God's heart is full of generosity. He's a gracious God, and we need to grasp that. God wants you to know this morning that he loves you. There is nothing you can do, if you are a Christian, to make him love you more, and there is nothing you can do to make him love you less.

And God's generosity flows into the whole world. He blesses those who are his people, and those who aren't. Every good thing in the world comes from the hand of God, whether it is acknowledged or not – it's what theologians call 'common grace'. Actually, God loves to give gifts to people. In Paul's evangelistic sermons, particularly when he is speaking to the Gentiles, he doesn't start with the Bible; he starts with creation (Acts 14 or 17). Paul argues, God made this whole world. He gives you rain, he loves to bless you, he's not a long way off and he wants to be found by you! God gives good things all the time to his children, and when we think about suffering, let's not forget all the good things that we enjoy from his hand. Every last thing that we enjoy that is good comes ultimately from the hand of our God. The Lord is good.

I used to play a game with my daughter when she was about two years old. She'd hide behind the chair, and I'd go in and say, 'Daddy's coming to look for Emmaus. Where's Emmaus? Is she behind the curtain?' And she'd shout, 'No, Daddy, I'm behind the chair!' 'Is she by the cupboard?' 'No, Daddy! I'm behind the chair!' 'Oh, is she round the corner?' 'No, Daddy, I'm behind the chair!' She must have thought, 'This man is stupid! I'm behind the chair!' And we think of God as hiding, but God, all the time, in his common grace, in all his gifts, in all his generosity, in the birth of every child, in every wonderful celebration, in every meal, in everything that happens in this wonderful world he has made, is saying, 'My arms are wide open – will you not come to me?' And instead of starting by telling unbelievers how bad they are, just tell them about the goodness of God. They will soon see what they need and reflect on that.

God's plans are inscrutable

The second thing I want you to notice, in verses 18–28, is that God's plans are inscrutable. In verse 17 the child is born. Verse 18 reports, 'The child grew, and one day he went out to his father, who was with the reapers.' There is a time gap between verses 17 and 18. We don't know how long the time gap was, so we don't know how old the little boy was. He's old enough to go out with his dad, but young enough to be carried up in the arms of one of the servants. His life up to this point has been pretty idyllic, I imagine. He's grown up on a farm. He's the apple of his mum and dad's eye, and from time to time Uncle Elisha probably comes and tells him stories of Israel. The day begins like any other normal day. But look at verses 19–20:

> He said to his father, 'My head! My head!'
> His father told a servant, 'Carry him to his mother.'
> After the servant had lifted him up and carried him to
> his mother, the boy sat on her lap until noon, and then
> he died.

Verses 17–20 are a mini-biography – he was born, he grew, he got sick and he died. Verse 20 must be one of the most poignant verses in the whole Bible. This little boy whom she has loved and doted on is taken from her. It shouldn't happen like that. Parents are supposed to be buried by their kids – not the other way around. And I guess for some of you today, that has been the greatest tragedy. Sometimes

God's ways are just puzzling. Sometimes we don't have an answer to what God is doing, do we?

I've been in Bath for about sixteen months now and have been working very closely with a guy called Clover. Don't ask me why he is called Clover – that just happens to be his name. He is in his thirties, and his wife Sarah died some years ago, leaving him with two little girls. He has been very brave, and the girls are exemplary, but a few months ago we heard that Clover had fallen in love with Melissa, a young lady in her twenties. And when it was announced in the church, everybody cheered and clapped: 'That's fantastic – isn't the Lord good!' He married Melissa about a month ago. But a few weeks before the wedding it was found that Melissa had cancer. It was cancer in the lung and probably elsewhere, and it looked as if it was very serious. The consultant said to them, 'Have a really, really, really good honeymoon, and when you come back, we'll talk about it.' You don't want to hear that, do you? Well, they had the wedding, they went on the honeymoon, they came back and the news was that the cancer was confined to just the lung. On Monday – two days ago – Melissa had the lung removed.

In the background of that, Clover has a brother called Neil, about the same age. Neil is married to Elaine. He is a pastor in Bristol and has two little boys. Elaine is terminally ill, and she probably doesn't have long to go. It's almost unbelievable. I've talked with Clover, we've wept together and I've said, 'What is God doing?' And sometimes you don't know! There are people who come up with all these easy solutions – 'Oh just pray about it. If you pray harder, you will be healed.' But we know that the world's not like that. We come to God, and he doesn't always give us the answer, and, actually, sometimes we wouldn't understand it if he did.

Some years ago I was a bit stressed, so my kids bought me a goldfish. Every morning he would swim up to me, and I'd talk to him. We had a great relationship, until I discovered that goldfish have a memory span of about five minutes. He hadn't got a clue who I was! Every time I met him, it was like the first time. Here's the point: the difference between his brain and mine is huge. He's in this tiny aquatic world, swimming round and round in circles, and I'm in this big wide world. I can go on the internet, make plans with people, communicate and read. The difference between his little brain and mine is so huge. And yet, the difference between my brain and our Creator's brain is even greater. You know, the one who made the heavens and holds the stars in space is God, and I am dust. And so, although Christians are precious in his sight, no wonder we can't understand his plans. And even if he explained them, we wouldn't always understand.

So what do we do? Well, look at what this woman did. I love this part of the story. I just love this woman. She is brilliant! She decides, 'I'm going to get to Elisha, no matter what – he's the man of God with the Word of God.' So, 'She went up and laid him on the bed of the man of God, then shut the door and went out' (verse 21). We need to remember that in that culture, normally, someone who dies is buried the same day. But she has a hope that this little boy hasn't seen the end of his life, that he's going to rise again. I'm not sure where she gets this hope from. Maybe she remembers Elijah had done something similar. She shuts the door to the room so that no-one can take the body out and bury him. And then she goes to her husband and says, 'Please send me one of the servants and a donkey so I can go to the man of God quickly and return.'

'Why go to him today?' he asks. 'It's not the New Moon or the Sabbath.' He's asking, 'What do you want to go to church for? It's not Sunday!' This bloke really doesn't get it! He doesn't even say, 'Where's my son? What's his headache like?' So, she kind of bypasses this discussion and 'She saddled the donkey and said to her servant, "Lead on"' (verse 24).

It's interesting if you look back to verse 23, when her husband says, 'What's going on?' She says, 'It is well.' In Hebrew she simply says, '*Shalom*', essentially, 'Everything is going to be OK! It is well.' It is that verse which inspired Horatio Spafford to write the hymn, 'It Is Well with My Soul'. He had lost four of his daughters at sea. And yet, he says, 'I know they are in God's hands. Everything is going to be OK, because ultimately this is in the hand of God.'

She got as far as Mount Carmel when Elisha saw her in the distance. He said to his servant Gehazi, 'Look! There's the Shunammite! Run to meet her and ask her, "Are you all right? Is your husband all right? Is your child all right?"' (verses 25–26). She sees Gehazi, but she doesn't stop until she reaches Elisha at the mountain. Gehazi wants to push her aside, 'but the man of God said, "Leave her alone!"' And in verse 28 she throws herself at his feet, and she clings to him: 'Did I ask you for a son, my lord? Didn't I tell you "Don't raise my hopes"?' In other words, he was God's gift that broke my heart.

Now what does the woman do? She runs as fast as a jet plane and gets to the man of God with the Word of God. What do we do? What do we do when life falls apart, when we are living in a broken world with broken hearts? We run to Jesus. Nothing is going to get in this woman's way – not the distance, not the husband, not the servant, nothing. I've got to get to Jesus. All your anxiety, all your care, bring to the mercy seat, leave it there. And when you get to Jesus, he won't necessarily tell you why. He won't give you an answer. But he will give you something far better than an answer – he will give you himself. He will embrace you, he will take you in his arms and he will say, 'It is well. Trust me.'

If my little five-year-old daughter comes off her scooter and hurts her knee, I don't look at her and think, 'This is a wonderful opportunity to educate her.' I don't hold her at arm's length and say, 'Darling, I want you to understand why it's painful. First of all, it's all to do with the law of physics. You were travelling at three miles per hour and you hit a curb at 73 degrees. If you had hit it any slower or if you had hit it at 78 degrees, you would have been OK! And it's all to do with physiology, the central nervous system has sent a message through the pain receptors in your knee to tell your brain that it hurts. Do you get that lesson? And as far as wanting a hug? Well, that's all to do with psychology . . .' Do I say that to her? No, no, no. I take her in my arms. I hug her, kiss her and say, 'Everything is going to be OK.'

That's what Jesus does. He doesn't give us an answer, because we don't live by explanations, we live by promises. The one who takes us in his arms, gathers us to himself and puts his strong embrace around us is the one who has nail-pinned hands. He's been there. He has tasted our sorrows. Forgive me for being personal here. My wife has struggled with illness for twenty-three years and she copes remarkably well. But there have been times where we have almost given up. There was a period that we described as 'the period of the attacks'. It was so painful that she couldn't bear to look at the light. She said it was like putting your hands in steam. The pain was overwhelming, and an attack would last for an hour! There was one day when we counted twenty-three attacks in a day. Just impossible. The Lord got us through it by his grace and the love of his people. But do you know, the thing that sustained us more than anything else is that we dwelt near Calvary, we dwelt near Jesus? We couldn't move away from that place; we needed Jesus. My friends, this morning, I can't answer why the things in your life are happening – just go to Jesus. If you have never been to him yet, go to him. Go to Jesus.

God's power is invincible

'Elisha said to Gehazi, "Tuck your cloak into your belt, take my staff in your hand and run. Don't greet anyone you meet . . ."' Just get to this boy! Get there! And so Gehazi lays the staff on the boy's face, but nothing happens. The woman and Elisha set off.

> When Elisha reached the house, there was the boy lying
> dead on his couch. He went in, shut the door on the two
> of them and prayed to the LORD. Then he got on the bed
> and lay on the boy, mouth to mouth, eyes to eyes, hands
> to hands. As he stretched himself out on him, the boy's
> body grew warm.
> (verses 32–34)

He understands that the boy is dead and he touches him. It's not magic – maybe because he is the prophet of life he's identifying with the body. It seems he is touching the child in order in some way to convey life. And then he prays and something seems to stir. So in verse 35: 'Elisha turned away and walked back and forth in the room and then got onto the bed and stretched out on him once more.' Then the boy sneezes! He's alive! And she goes in, and Elisha gives the boy back to her (verses 36–37). God has broken the power of death. What on earth are we to make of that?

First of all, let me say that this is not a model for ministry. By which I mean, we don't read this story and say, 'Well, obviously if somebody dies, all you have to do is pray hard enough and they'll get healed.' Just as this story is not saying that in the tragedy of childlessness, if you pray harder and believe more, God will give you a child. I'm guessing this morning that some of you struggle with the pain of childlessness, and the Lord is with you in that. Can God do miracles? Of course, he can. Can God heal? I believe that 100%. But that's not what this story is saying. Actually, miracles are comparatively rare in the Bible, and the miracle of raising the dead is particularly rare. In the Old Testament there are only three occasions: Elijah, Elisha and post-mortem Elisha. In the New Testament Jesus does it three times, Peter does it, Paul does it, and that's the lot! There is an incident around the resurrection of Jesus, but that's all the examples in the whole of the Bible. This is not a common thing. So, the conclusion is not to pray harder and your loved one will be raised from the dead. Can God do it? Yes! Will he do it? Maybe not. What is this passage telling us? Well, it's pointing us forward.

If you leave Shunem and travel two miles north, you will come to another little village. Anyone know what it is called? It's called the village of Nain. We read in Luke 7:11–13:

> Soon afterwards, Jesus went to a town called Nain, and his disciples and a large crowd went along with him. As he approached the town gate, a dead person was being carried out – the only son of his mother, and she was a widow. And a large crowd from the town was with her. When the Lord saw her, his heart went out to her and he said, 'Don't cry.'

Jesus' heart is full of compassion, and yet he says, 'Don't cry.' If he didn't do what he is about to do, that would be a horrendous thing to say. Of course she cried – but Jesus knows what comes next:

> Then he went up and touched the bier they were carrying him on, and the bearers stood still. He said, 'Young man, I say to you, get up!' The dead man sat up and began to talk, and Jesus gave him back to his mother.

You read that story and you can't miss the similarities! Remember what we said in the beginning about the type and the antitype? But the differences are what stick out in my mind. Elisha doesn't know what is going on. He sends the staff, and that doesn't work. He sends Gehazi, and he can't do it. Elisha himself can't do it. He prays and lies on the body again, and only then does Yahweh heal. Yahweh is the one who raised the boy in the Old Testament. Here it is Jesus. There is no messing about, there is no rigmarole, there's no misunderstanding – Jesus walks straight up, he touches the boy and the boy jumps up. So, here is the difference. Jesus is the Lord of life; he's the one who is the conqueror of death. 'In the beginning was the Word, and the Word was with God, and the Word was God . . . In him was life, and that life was the light of all mankind' (John 1:1, 4).

The power of Christ is invincible. Elisha can pray, and God can do a miracle through it; Jesus has the power of life. This miracle looks forward to Jesus. And then it looks forward, even beyond Jesus, to the last pages of the Bible. Turn to Revelation 21. Every miracle in the Bible is intended to take us to this passage. Every miracle is a foretaste of what God is going to do one day to the whole universe. You know when you go to the cinema and you see a preview of a film and you think, 'I want to see that!' The miracles are the previews! This is what is going to happen one day:

> I saw the Holy City, a new Jerusalem, coming down out of heaven from God . . . And I heard a loud voice from the throne saying, 'Look! God's dwelling-place is now among the people, and he will dwell with them. They will be his people, and God himself will be with them and be their God. He will wipe every tear from their eyes. There will be no more death or mourning or crying or pain, for the old order of things has passed away.'
> (verses 2–4)

Every miracle points to that day of redemption when pain is a thing of the past. In the meantime, God doesn't always give us the answers, but he gives us himself. He doesn't always wipe away the tears, but one day he will. For now, Jesus is with us, he is for us and he is the Lord of life. Serve in his strength, even in the darkness, and whatever happens, say, 'It is well with my soul.'

Note

1. See Dale Ralph Davis, *2 Kings: The Power and the Fury* (Christian Focus, 2005).

Faith under Pressure – The Son of Man: Christ-Centred Faith in a Power-Hungry World

by *John Risbridger*

John Risbridger is Chair of Keswick Ministries and serves as Minister and Team Leader at Above Bar Church in Southampton. After coming to Christ at a young age, he studied mathematics and economics in Nottingham and was very active in the Christian Union. He spent ten years on the staff of UCCF after five years in NHS management. He has a deep love of expository Bible teaching, along with a particular interest in the theology and practice of Christian worship. He is married to Alison and they have two daughters.

Faith under Pressure – The Son of Man: Christ-Centred Faith in a Power-Hungry World: Daniel 6 – 7

I wonder if you've ever played one of those word association games at a party. Someone says a word, and you have to say the next word that comes into your head and then explain what the connection is, however bizarre the link may be. Well, I don't think there is much doubt what most Christians would say if we played the game with the word 'Daniel'. Let's try. If I say 'Daniel', what word comes to mind? Hands up if it had something to do with lions? This is certainly the most famous chapter in the book of Daniel. However, rather than going through verse by verse, I want us to reflect instead on how we might read this familiar chapter.

How might we read Daniel 6?

Do we read it as a contrast between the weakness of the powerful and the strength of the weak? Certainly, that is a striking feature, captured by the way in which the text alternates between the *powerless* Daniel who seems so strong and the *powerful* Darius who is ineffectual and easily manipulated.[1]

Do we read it as a model of the praying life? Well, certainly Daniel is a great model of a believer who wouldn't give up praying, whatever the cost.

Do we read it as a model of workplace integrity? Well, Daniel was outstandingly good and conscientious at his job. As a pastor, I love meeting people who love their job and do it well. Too often pastors only seem interested in persuading people to be pastors – or failing that, missionaries – but the God of the Bible commissioned us to work in creation, and the New Testament tells us that God values good work and calls us to do it for him and his glory.

Daniel is so good and so conscientious, that his colleagues are jealous of his success, and they attempt to discredit him, but nothing that they throw at him will stick:

> The chief ministers and the satraps tried to find grounds
> for charges against Daniel in his conduct of government
> affairs, but they were unable to do so. They could find
> no corruption in him, because he was trustworthy and
> neither corrupt nor negligent.
> (verse 4)

He was trustworthy and faithful. He was the kind of guy you could depend on to get the job done properly. When the boss left something in Daniel's hands, he could be confident that Daniel wouldn't give him half-baked effort and a bunch of excuses. Neither was he corrupt. The chief ministers and the satraps couldn't even find small irregularities in his conduct – the big picture *and* the details were transparent and clean. He was not negligent or careless. He didn't cut corners to get himself off the hook. He made sure things were done properly and in order. But he had one Achilles heel that everyone knew about, and that was his unswerving loyalty to God: 'Finally these men said, "We will never find any basis for charges against this man Daniel unless it has something to do with the law of his God"' (verse 5). In the end, the law of Daniel's God would come before the law of the Medes and Persians.

So, Daniel is a great model of godliness in the workplace. He wasn't thinking he'd missed his vocation and should have been a priest. He knew God had called him to civil service in the empire and had kept him there. He was very open about his faith. He didn't leave his trust in God in the car park when he got to work. And his integrity was outstanding, because he was expressing his faith through his work. He was not the kind of believer who thought shoddiness at work was OK, because what really mattered was his Christian service. His work *was* his Christian service.

Daniel is a great model for us to reflect on. It is so crucial that we don't give in to the idea that all serious Christians should end up in 'full-time Christian work' (other than in the sense that we are all full-time Christian workers!). God calls us to work out our discipleship 24/7, in every sphere of human life. And, for most of us, most of the time, that means in the workplace.

Do we read this chapter as a model of workplace evangelism? After all, Darius ends up making a remarkable confession of faith in the God of Israel at the end of the chapter. But if the lesson is that you have to be fed to the lions in order to win your boss for Jesus, that might not be altogether encouraging!

Do we read this chapter as a model of courage and a promise of deliverance? 'Dare to be a Daniel,' we used to sing in our Sunday school classes. Daniel's faith was an immensely courageous faith. He continues to pray even though it may cost him his life – unlike many of us who give up praying if it will cost us a vaguely interesting programme on TV. And this courageous faith was rewarded with a stunning deliverance: the mouths of the lions were shut and he was unharmed. Without doubt, that is the heart of the passage. But that is also where the real problem is. How do we interpret this famous and familiar story? God does not always rescue from death people of courageous faith who put their trust in him. Just think of all the Christians subsequently fed to the lions in Roman amphitheatres. By the most conservative estimates, at least 1,200 believers are martyred each year;[2] some say the figure is much higher.

So, is there a bigger picture that can help us grasp this passage? Well, I think this chapter gives us *a window onto the ultimate deliverance.* Just as the innocent Daniel was a victim of betrayal and conspiracy, so the sinless Jesus was betrayed and conspired against. Just as Daniel was arrested in the place of prayer, so Jesus was arrested in Gethsemane, the garden where he prayed. Just as Darius found no fault with Daniel, so Pilate found no fault with Jesus. Just as Daniel was thrown to the pit of lions, so Jesus was led away to the cross – the place of death, or execution. Just as the lions' pit was covered with a stone and sealed, so Jesus' tomb was closed with a great stone and a Roman seal. And yet, as Daniel was pulled from the pit of lions at the first light of dawn, so on the first Easter morning it was found that the tomb of Jesus was empty, and he appeared to Mary and the disciples. He was swallowed up by the jaws of death, but he broke them in his resurrection; death itself was defeated. So, although God's people still suffer across the world today, they know that a glorious deliverance awaits them too. A deliverance not merely into more years of exile, but into new creation life, in which they share God's everlasting joy!

It is with that eternal perspective that the story concludes, surprisingly enough, through the words of Darius himself in verses 25–27:

> Then King Darius wrote to all the nations and peoples of every language in all the earth:
>
> 'May you prosper greatly!
> 'I issue a decree that in every part of my kingdom people must fear and reverence the God of Daniel.
>
> 'For he is the living God
> and he endures for ever;

his kingdom will not be destroyed,
his dominion will never end.
He rescues and he saves;
he performs signs and wonders
in the heavens and on the earth.
He has rescued Daniel
from the power of the lions.'

And it is confident assurance of the God who saves that provides the bridge into chapters 7 – 12, which bring us a series of visions preparing God's people for the severe suffering still to come. The thing that will sustain them is the confidence that their God is the 'living God' who 'rescues' and who 'saves' eternally.

God saves and his kingdom prevails (Daniel 7)

Daniel looks, at first sight, like a book of two halves:

Chapters 1 – 6: stories of faith in a time of exile
Chapters 7 – 12: visions of the future beyond the exile

But there is something else to notice. In Daniel 2:4 the language changes from Hebrew (Israel's language) to Aramaic (the international language of the empire), and doesn't switch back until the end of chapter 7.[3] That gives us an overlapping structure, which puts chapter 7, with its vision of the Son of Man, right at the heart of the book. So what do you do if you read the stories of spectacular deliverance in Daniel 1 – 6 and find yourself thinking, 'That was great for them, but so often life isn't like that'? Think of the suffering Christians of North Korea, Syria, Afghanistan and Iraq for whom no deliverance is in sight. Maybe *you* took a stand for Jesus in your workplace and it resulted, not in promotion, like Daniel and his friends, but in trouble. Maybe you live your life under the cloud of a manipulative boss, a difficult spouse, a controlling colleague – and there seems to be no escape. Maybe our nation is on a trajectory away from freedom of religion towards the persecution of religion, and things are getting darker. What do you do to find hope in a world where suffering continues?

Daniel's answer is that you don't stop reading his book at chapter 6! Because the visions of the remaining chapters are all about living as the people of God in a power-hungry world where empires rise and fall, suffering continues and deliverance is far away. Let's plunge into chapter 7.

Daniel's dream

A power-hungry world (verses 1–8)
Chapter 7 begins with a vision of four terrifying beasts coming out of the sea. According to verse 17, the four beasts represent four kings or kingdoms:

> Four great beasts, each different from the others, came up out of the sea.
>
> The first was like a lion, and it had the wings of an eagle. I watched until its wings were torn off and it was lifted

from the ground so that it stood on two feet like a human being, and the mind of a human was given to it.
(verses 3–4)

If the four beasts parallel the four parts of the great statue in Nebuchadnezzar's dream in chapter 2, then this is about Nebuchadnezzar and Babylon. The lion and the eagle speak respectively of pride and power – both of which Babylon possessed in spades! But in this vision, the proud, powerful empire is humbled, its powerful eagle wings torn off and 'the mind of a human given to it' – probably a reference to Nebuchadnezzar's experience in chapter 4.

Look at the second beast in verse 5:

And there before me was a second beast, which looked like a bear. It was raised up on one of its sides, and it had three ribs in its mouth between its teeth. It was told, 'Get up and eat your fill of flesh!'

Syrian bears could weigh up to 250 kg, so again this is an alarming image. The bear is devouring the last pieces of its previous catch, the ribs still in its mouth, while rising to begin the next hunt. Its voracious appetite is never satisfied.

The third beast is described in verse 6:

After that, I looked, and there before me was another beast, one that looked like a leopard. And on its back it had four wings like those of a bird. This beast had four heads, and it was given authority to rule.

A flying leopard would be a terrifying beast – savage, swift and lethal. The four heads are associated with its authority to rule and probably represent four kings ruling in this kingdom.

The fourth beast is different. It isn't like any animal, but it is 'terrifying and frightening and very powerful'. It has ten horns, symbols of strength and power, which probably represent ten kings, followed by the 'boastful' horn of verse 8. Look at verses 7–8:

> After that, in my vision at night I looked, and there before me was a fourth beast – terrifying and frightening and very powerful. It had large iron teeth; it crushed and devoured its victims and trampled underfoot whatever was left. It was different from all the former beasts, and it had ten horns.
>
> While I was thinking about the horns, there before me was another horn, a little one, which came up among them; and three of the first horns were uprooted before it. This horn had eyes like the eyes of a human being and a mouth that spoke boastfully.

In verse 28, 'I, Daniel, was deeply troubled by my thoughts, and my face turned pale.' That is the effect these images are meant to have. They reveal the dark realities of a power-hungry world, in which human power structures tend to degenerate into self-serving, destructive regimes, unless God speaks into them by his servants. We see it around the world today in brutal dictatorships; we see it in the degeneration of democracies into mere theatres of celebrity and self-interested contests for power; we see it in the voracious greed of some of the multinationals asset stripping weaker nations; we see it in churches divided by power disputes and personality cults. This is a horrible vision – and it's meant to be!

There's a big debate about which empires these beasts represent. It is possible that they are Babylon, Media, Persia and Greece. This view usually goes with the idea that the book of Daniel belongs to the second century BC and is artificially projected back into the sixth-century exile. The alternative is the traditional view that they are Babylon, Medo-Persia, Greece and Rome, often with the little horn representing a final 'anti-Christ' type of figure. I find the first view just too problematic, but I also think it's too simple to say that the fourth beast is Rome. For starters, what exactly do we mean by Rome? The Western Empire which fell in AD 476, or the Eastern Empire which continued until the fall of Constantinople nearly 1,000 years later? And Roman influence is still very much alive through its language, its script, its definitive impact on the sciences and on law. So is the fourth beast dead or alive? Also, the emphasis here is that this beast is not just another empire like the others. It is a 'different' kingdom that defies easy categorization (verse 7b). Perhaps it is best seen as representing all the subsequent manifestations of human empire and global domination, from Rome to the end of history as we know it.

But from this terrifying depiction of a power-hungry world, Daniel's vision shifts to an even more awesome picture of God's heavenly rule.

The heavenly court (verses 9–10)
'As I looked, "thrones were set in place [note, there is more than one], and the Ancient of Days [that is, God, not as a frail old man, but as the awesome ruler of history] took his seat [notice, the beasts do not lead him to panic; he is calmly seated and gloriously sovereign]. His clothing was as white as snow; the hair of his head was white like wool [so he is absolutely pure, just and holy]. His throne was flaming with fire, and its wheels were all ablaze. A river of fire was flowing, coming out from before him [this fire is his holy wrath against sin, being poured out in consuming judgment]. Thousands upon thousands attended him; ten thousand times ten thousand stood before him [all of a sudden these earthly empires which have terrified us are looking small and rather ordinary]. The court was seated, and the books were opened [God the Judge is ready to step in, in perfect justice, to put things right]."'

If we trembled before the vision of human empires, how much more should we tremble before this breathtaking vision of divine sovereignty and justice? Who can stand when God has his books open? Who can survive when holy wrath is flowing from his throne?

The enthronement of the Son of Man (verses 11–14)
For all our human pride and self-importance, no king, no empire and none of us can survive the fury of the righteous wrath of God. Verse 11 tells about the end of the fourth, climactic beast:

Then I continued to watch because of the boastful words the horn was speaking. I kept looking until the beast was slain and its body destroyed and thrown into the blazing fire.

As for the other beasts, by this time they had already been neutralized, though they had survived in some form for a short time (verse 12). So is there any hope at all for human beings? Is there anyone who can stand before the justice of an all-powerful God?

The stunning answer is that there is! Verse 13: 'In my vision at night I looked, and there before me was one like a son of man [a human being, but though human, he is doing something very God-like; he is . . .] coming with the clouds of heaven.' Where is he coming? Not to earth as we often assume, but to heaven! 'He approached the Ancient of Days and was led into his presence' (verse 13b). But rather than be consumed by the fire of God's holiness, he is vindicated, enthroned forever and worshipped by the nations:

He was given authority, glory and sovereign power; all nations and peoples of every language worshipped him. His dominion is an everlasting dominion that will not pass away, and his kingdom is one that will never be destroyed. (verse 14)

Remember that there was more than one throne in verse 13, and now he is entering heaven to sit down and share in

the everlasting reign of God! This is the glorious enthronement of the Son of Man!

Who is this Son of Man? Well, perhaps at some level
this vision did give faithful Israelites a hope of vindication,
but these verses cry out for a fulfilment that goes much
further. If we believe that the whole of Scripture shares a
common divine author, I cannot see how we can miss the
most obvious answer! There was a man who chose to call
himself the Son of Man, in whose life God's kingdom
reign was established; a man whose flawless obedience led
him to death on the cross for the sins of the world and yet
who was gloriously vindicated by God through his resurrection; a man who, when his work was completed,
ascended to the Father to rule in incomparable majesty at
his right hand.

His name is Jesus. He is the true and ultimate Son of
Man. All authority has been given to him forever, and every
knee shall bow before him and every tongue will confess
him to be Lord. Our only proper response is: 'Hallelujah!'
The only faith that sustains hope in a power-hungry,
suffering world is faith in Christ, because all power has
finally been entrusted to him.

Catch a glimpse of him and earthly empires will be cut
down to size.

Catch a glimpse of him and you'll know God will have
the last word.

Catch a glimpse of him and you'll know it is worth
remaining faithful.

The meaning of Daniel's dream (verses 15–28)

The vindication of the people of God

We have jumped ahead into some of this already, but take a look at the summary in verses 15–18:

> I, Daniel, was troubled in spirit, and the visions that passed through my mind disturbed me. I approached one of those standing there and asked him the meaning of all this.
>
> So he told me and gave me the interpretation of these things: 'The four great beasts are four kings that will rise from the earth. But the holy people of the Most High will receive the kingdom and will possess it for ever – yes, for ever and ever.'

The surprise is that the kingdom is possessed by 'the holy people of the Most High', whereas in verse 14 it is possessed by the Son of Man. However, the key thing is that these verses do not *replace* the vision; they *interpret* its meaning. The vision is about the enthronement of the Son of Man, which, in full New Testament high definition, is the ascension and glorification of Christ. The interpretation of the vision is about what the enthronement of the Son of Man means for the people who look to him as their glorious head and representative – the holy people of the Most High. And the glorious truth we discover is that they are caught up in his victory: his vindication is their vindication; the judgment in favour of him is a judgment in favour of them; the kingdom given to him is finally possessed by them!

The fourth beast and the 'boastful horn'
In verses 19–21 Daniel wants to zoom in on the fourth beast, the ten horns and the boastful horn that was opposing God's people. He receives this explanation in verse 23:

> The fourth beast is a fourth kingdom that will appear
> on earth. It will be different from all the other kingdoms
> and will devour the whole earth, trampling it down and
> crushing it.

Notice this beast is 'different', global and destructive. It is like Rome at its worst, but even more so: the culmination of all it represented.

Look at verses 24–25:

> The ten horns are ten kings who will come from this
> kingdom. After them another king will arise, different
> from the earlier ones; he will subdue three kings. He will
> speak against the Most High and oppress his holy people
> and try to change the set times and the laws. The holy
> people will be delivered into his hands for a time, times
> and half a time.

This boastful horn is, above everything, an anti-God figure. He is blaspheming God, persecuting his people and seeking to undermine the practice of their faith. Many attempts have been made to explain verse 25b, but the point may well be simple: this powerful anti-God figure will have his time, during which God's people will suffer dreadfully. But it will not last forever.

Coming suffering which will not last forever
Look at verses 26–27:

> But the court will sit, and his power will be taken away
> and completely destroyed for ever. Then the sovereignty,
> power and greatness of all the kingdoms under heaven
> will be handed over to the holy people of the Most High.
> His kingdom will be an everlasting kingdom, and all rulers
> will worship and obey him.

This is the ultimate deliverance of which all the others in Daniel are pictures.

So, for faithful Jews returning from exile, this was a warning of more suffering to come and an assurance that God would see to their final vindication. Justice is in his hands. For God's people today, here is a warning that suffering will continue until the very end of the age. Foreshadowings of the 'anti-God' regime of the little horn continue through history, but will find their culmination in the final terror of the one whom the New Testament calls 'the anti-Christ' or 'the man of lawlessness'.

But although suffering continues in many forms and may yet intensify, it will not continue forever, because the Son of Man is at the Father's side: crucified, risen, ascended and sovereign. His victory has already, in principle, been won. Judgment has already been passed in favour of him, and therefore the outcome of history is certain: we, his people, will possess the kingdom and reign with him! Now we suffer; then we shall reign, for sure. This is the faith by which we can live in a power-hungry world where suffering continues: faith in Jesus – the glorified, risen, vindicated, ascended Son of Man – 'who for the joy that was set before him endured the cross, scorning its shame, and sat down at the right hand of the throne of God' (Hebrews 12:2).

Notes

1. A possible outline of Daniel 6:
   Daniel's integrity (verses 1–5)
   Darius – the danger of manipulation (verses 6–9)
   Daniel's prayers (verses 10–11)
   Darius – the trap of vanity (verses 12–18)
   Daniel's deliverance (verses 19–24)
   Darius – the dawning of faith (verses 25–28).
2. See Open Doors: www.opendoorsuk.org.
3. Most likely, the writer intended chapters 2 – 7 to be read by the nations, with their stories of the victory of Israel's God, while the opening and close of the book were specifically for Israel.

The Lecture

Faithful, Fruitful and Free – Confident Disciples on Today's Frontlines

by Mark Greene

Mark Greene used to work in advertising and is prepared to admit it. He's now Executive Director of the London Institute for Contemporary Christianity. Mark is a champion for mission in ordinary life, speaks widely, and has written a number of books and resources, including *Thank God It's Monday*, *The Great Divide*, the ground-breaking *Imagine: How We Can Reach the UK*, *Fruitfulness on the Frontline* which has a supporting DVD resource for small groups, and jointly with Antony Billington, this year's Keswick Bible Study Guide: *The Whole of Life for Christ*. He is married to Katrina and they have two sons and a daughter – Matt, Tomas and Anna-Marie.

Faithful, Fruitful and Free – Confident Disciples on Today's Frontlines

I know that church attendance has declined enormously over the last ten years, but I have to say that I have never been so excited about the potential of God's people to make a transformative impact on our nation for Christ as I am now. There are a number of reasons for that, but one of them is that virtually every day I hear a new story of God at work in fresh ways in people's lives.

Still, the missional challenge is formidable. There are around 63 million people living in our nation, and around 59 million of those people don't know Jesus. Today around 6.1% of the UK population go to church once a month or more. It's a small percentage, but 6.1% of a UK population of 63 million is 3,843,000 people – and that's 3,842,988 more than Jesus started with!

It's a lot of people. And between us, in an average week, we probably connect to at least 90% of the people in the country – through family; through the schools and colleges Christian kids go to; the hospitals, shops and offices Christian workers serve in; the clubs Christian people are part of; the shops they frequent; the residential homes they live in. We have the people to reach our nation.

Why have Christians lost their confidence?

As you are no doubt aware, one of the reasons cited for the decline in conversions over the last decade has been a marked decline in Christians' confidence in the gospel. Lots of reasons have been given for this: the scandals that have affected the reputation of the church; the view that we are judgmental, narrow-minded and homophobic; the suspicion of organized religions in general; the challenges of living in a multi-faith culture; the rise of consumerism and so on.

Many suggest that we lack confidence in the gospel because we find it difficult to defend intellectually the truth claims we make: that the Bible is a reliable historical document; that Jesus was a real historical figure; that Christianity is the only way; that the Bible provides a reliable framework for living life well; that it has something vital to say about working well, parenting well, playing well, educating well, caring well, running a business well, managing people well, running a country well; that the gospel of Jesus Christ is not just a message of personal salvation, but a manifesto for the regeneration of every area of public, national and international life.

However, we can have confidence in God's Word. Certainly in the particular areas that I have spent a bit of time looking at – work and organizations – the leading secular research seems to confirm what the Word of God had already told us.

So, for example, we did not need Jim Collins in his ground-breaking, hugely influential, rigorously researched book *Good to Great*[1] to tell us that one of the two key qualities of an outstanding workplace leader is humility. We already knew it from the example of the one,

> who, being in very nature God,
>> did not consider equality with God something
>>> to be used to his own advantage;
> rather, he made himself nothing
>> by taking the very nature of a servant.
> (Philippians 2:6–7)

We did not need Fred Kiel's recent quantitative research to tell us that a key indicator of long-term organizational success might be the character of the leaders.[2] But it is helpful that he has.

We do not need the many tomes on the decline of trust to confirm that improving the quality of relationships between people might generate higher levels of employee engagement, satisfaction and productivity. We have already been told that loving our neighbour is one of the two great commandments.

The same applies to other areas. Do gospel-shaped initiatives make a positive difference to reoffending rates among juvenile offenders? Do gospel-shaped initiatives make a positive difference to reoffending rates among adult prisoners? Do gospel-shaped initiatives radically reduce the number of people taken into state care? Do gospel-shaped initiatives help severely indebted people? Yes, they do.

The gospel is good news for the lost; good news for the poor; good news for nations; good news for towns, neighbourhoods, churches, workplaces, appraisal systems, leadership training, employee relations, financial services, education and law enforcement. You can find lots of helpful material on these issues, and they are all important to building confidence, but they aren't the only ones.

So I would like to share some of the things we at LICC[3] have been learning over the last eight years about helping people grow more confident in their calling to be God's people out in everyday life, out on what we call our *frontlines* – the places where we naturally engage with people who don't know Jesus in the course of our daily lives – our workplace, the gym, Weight Watchers, the school gate, the supermarket.

How does confidence grow?

Let me tell you about a woman who is a member of a small Baptist church in the West Midlands. Thelma is ninety-three, and not quite as fleet of foot as she was when she was eighty-nine. She does a few things in the church, but she doesn't really think she has a mission field, a frontline where she can minister to those who don't know Jesus. But her pastor showed her a DVD we produced, and suddenly Thelma realized that she does have a frontline, she does have a mission field – she had one all along, but she just couldn't see it.

Her frontline is the convenience store down her road run by an Asian family. It's a place where she goes regularly and engages with people she already knows. And so it is that throughout the winter – come rain, hail, sleet or snow – despite her friends pleading entreaties to 'Please, please, let us do your shopping for you', Thelma goes to minister to the people God has given her. And she's excited to still be working with God, and for God, in his great plans.

Don't we all want to be Thelmas, still going for it with God when we're ninety-three?

Don't we want to be Thelmas now?

Confidence grows when we realize God has already given us a place to minister and people to minister to. Confidence grows when we know where our mission field is.

Are you fruitful?

Confidence grows when you see results, when you see fruit. I wonder if we see fruit. And I wonder what we think fruit is.

A few years ago I began working with a group of Scots – mainly in their late twenties/early thirties, hand-picked by Mission Scotland[4] as people who might have the potential to become a SWAT team for workplace ministry north of the border. There was an actress, a banker, a housewife, a former civil servant, a jewellery shop sales-man, a teacher, a head teacher and a project manager.

As we began, we noticed something. None of these highly competent, well-taught people – despite their passion for the workplace and being involved in fine churches – thought they had anything to offer anyone else or that they were doing anything particularly special in their own workplace. They were confident workers, but not confident disciples

One of them was a head teacher who had rescued two failing primary schools in Glasgow from closure, and was in the process of turning a third one from a good school into an outstanding one. How could it be that she thought she had nothing to offer? She'd had a positive impact on the lives of over 300 children; she'd had a positive impact on the lives of the parents and the wider families of over 300 children; she'd had a positive impact on the staff in those schools; she'd had a positive impact on the communities the schools were in because a good school generates community pride and hope. The problem was: she hadn't had that many direct evangelistic conversations.

When I visited her school, she began to tell me some stories. Let me tell you one of them:

Something bad has happened in the school and a ten-year-old boy, who has often been in trouble, is accused by one, then two, then three staff of having perpetrated the offence. He loses his temper and runs off into the school field. The head teacher is summoned, and she goes out to the field to talk to him. He tells her, 'It wasn't me, Miss. It wasn't me. I didn't do it. But they wouldn't listen.' She believes him. She walks him back to the school buildings, makes an enquiry and then goes to talk to the three staff. She tells them that the boy is innocent. To her, every child is special, every child is worth the trouble, even the children who are trouble. The three staff apologize to the boy. Subsequently, the boy who did the deed confessed and also apologized to the boy.

What happened here? Yes, justice has been done. Yes, the boy has been protected, vindicated and honoured; he has been given a second chance; he has experienced the sweetness of justice and he has discovered what it feels like when your past does not determine your future. And the staff have been taught. They have tasted Jesus' ways and found them good.

And yes, they all know the head teacher is a Christian.

But the most astonishing aspect of this story to me is that the teachers apologized! You see, when the head teacher arrived at the school, she told the staff, parents and pupils that she would make decisions and she would make mistakes. She told them that if they didn't like a decision, they should talk to her about it, and if she was wrong, she'd apologize and do something about it.

In other words, this head teacher had created and modelled a Matthew 18 forgiveness culture. She had invited them to behave in the ways of the kingdom. And once this head teacher had seen that teaching people the ways of Jesus was kingdom work, she realized that what she had been doing was actually worth talking about.

For many Christians, including every person in that group of well-taught people, their view of what constitutes 'good' and worth sharing had been defined too narrowly to evangelistic conversations. So they felt they hadn't been doing anything for God; they felt that God hadn't been working in them; they felt unfruitful, discouraged, frustrated and guilty.

Well, evangelism is vital, and it is very easy to lose evangelistic intentionality in the long haul that is ministry on our daily frontlines, but direct evangelistic activity is not the only criterion of faithfulness or fruitfulness.

We realized that we needed to help people see that in the Bible, fruitfulness covered more areas than just evangelism. And so we developed the **6Ms**, six overall ways in which God might be at work in and through his people:

How might I . . .
Model godly character
Make good work
Minister grace and love
Mould culture
Be a Mouthpiece for truth and justice
Be a Messenger of the gospel

So, seeing the Spirit ripen godly qualities in our lives is fruit that God delights in; making good work in the power of the Spirit to the glory of God is fruit that God delights in; ministering grace and love and moulding the culture of our workplace, gym or school gate to make it reflect kingdom values is fruit that God is interested in. Being a mouthpiece for truth and justice – not just standing up against systemic injustice, but snuffing out gossip in a church or ensuring the right person gets the credit for the work done – is good fruit. And so surely is being a messenger of the gospel – taking the opportunity to bring a biblical perspective to the conversation, talking about the difference Jesus has made in our life and helping someone understand what Jesus has done for them and how they can come to know him – that's fruit too.

It's all fruit. These six things work together. They add power and authenticity to our words. So, if you stand up for truth and justice, your colleague is much more likely to believe in a God of justice; if you minister grace and love, your golfing buddy who has just lost his father is much more likely to believe in a God of grace and love.

What this framework has done for people is to enable them to see how God is already working in and through them, and that breeds excitement. Confidence grows when you can see how you are already fruitful and have a clear sense of how you might be – when you have a goal to aim at. Confidence grows because you see that God is alive and working, and is already with you. Confidence grows when there's a sense of exhilaration about our relationship with God.

And as my confidence grows, I talk more about Jesus, because now I have a number of stories about how God has worked in my life – not just how I became a Christian, but how he is working now. I can witness to how he has rescued me and given me a fresh purpose, and I can witness to how he helped me last week.

Are you asking the right question?

Now one of the interesting things we've discovered is that if you ask the right question of almost anyone who's been a Christian for a while, then you discover that God has indeed been at work in and through them in remarkable ways.

A while back I was with a small group of around fifteen men from my church, and a man called Andy Gardner asked this question: What are you good at in the Lord in your work, on your frontline?

I love that question. Instead of assuming that Christians are unfruitful and ineffective and just need to be cajoled and challenged, Andy assumed something radically different. Theologically, he assumed that God had been at work in their lives. He assumed God would not waste any opportunity to help them grow or to work missionally through their daily lives, even if they weren't sharply aware of it. He assumed they're doing something right.

Often many people, not in paid church work, think they are second-class Christians, and that what they are doing isn't either significant or gleamingly holy. Yes, we expect that a group of people who've been on a ten-day ministry trip will have something to say about what God did. But do we have the same expectation that God might be working in our people on their frontlines?

And here's something that Andy didn't assume. He didn't assume that there would be only one kind of fruit. Still, when Andy asked us the question, 'What are you good at in the Lord in your work?', this being southern England and a Christian gathering, fourteen voices did not immediately pipe up. But interestingly, by the end everyone had spoken.

The first was Kirk. He told us, 'I'm part of the armed protection team at No 10. I protect the Prime Minister. As you can imagine, it's a pretty macho team, and there's often been a bit of conflict. And over the years I've found I've been pretty good at bringing people together.' That's all he said.

Someone in the room replied, 'You have a ministry of reconciliation.' And you should have seen his face – a smile the width of Kansas. And of course, he does have a ministry of reconciliation. He's a peacemaker, teaching people to forgive one another and live in the ways of Jesus.

He hadn't really clocked what God had been doing until he was asked the question and someone else helped him to see the significance of his answer. When someone put what he was doing in a biblical category, named it like that, honoured it, then suddenly he's full of joy, because now he knows that God is interested in this. Now he knows that

God is working through him, and you could see his confidence grow.

This is how you form a confident disciple-making community: enable people not only to tell their stories, but to name what God is doing and the lessons to be learned and transferred. Help them read their lives through biblical lenses and see how their actions conform to biblical standards.

Interestingly, I discovered later that his actions didn't only improve relationships and morale, but also improved security. Apparently, when you go into a life-and-death live-ammunition situation, it's absolutely imperative that you completely trust the rest of the team to do exactly what they are meant to do. Any smidgen of doubt can cause the kind of minuscule delay that can be lethal. Teaching forgiveness made the team stronger and contributed to the increased security of the Prime Minister.

The gospel has something to contribute to every situation.

So one of the ways we empower our people is by assuming that the Holy Spirit is working in them, and trying to help them see what God is already doing. It's a posture of positive expectation of God. God has, through Christ, transferred us from the dominion of darkness to the kingdom of his beloved Son; God has made us new creatures in Christ. 'Therefore, if anyone is in Christ, the new creation has come: the old has gone, the new is here!' (2 Corinthians 5:17). And we are not only new creations with new capacities; we have a God who is working to conform us more and more to the likeness of his Son. His beloved Holy Spirit is ripening fruit in us, enlivening the Word, guiding, interceding for us and empowering us. Given all that, isn't it quite likely that God would be working in us in some way?

Do you have a positive expectation of God?

Begin to build that positive expectation any Sunday, or in any home group or in any conversation, by asking the questions: 'What have you seen God doing recently? What has God been teaching you recently?'

So confidence grows when we recognize where our frontline is, when we have a clear sense of what godly fruit looks like, when we see godly fruit in ourselves and when we help one another to see fruit. Confidence also grows when we encourage one another, because we are telling each other, 'our frontline is important', 'what you do there is important'. As Hebrews puts it, 'Let us consider how we may spur one another on towards love and good deeds, not giving up meeting together, as some are in the habit of doing, but *encouraging one another* – and all the more as you see the Day approaching' (Hebrews 10:24–25, emphasis added).

Other translations say, 'spur one another', 'goad one another', 'provoke one another'. You arrive on Sunday morning at church and look around and see who you can provoke. Another translation is 'incite'. Incited anyone to religious goodness recently?

But there is a danger in a model like the 6Ms that we just burden ourselves with a whole new set of hurdles to jump over, a whole new set of things to feel guilty about. No, the 6Ms are not a new set of hurdles, but a trigger for our imagination and a spur for our prayers.

How do you picture God?

Beyond that, whether we are beset by false guilt and failure in our daily discipleship, or a sense of confident, purposeful freedom, may well depend on our picture of the character of God and his expectations. Our metaphors shape our imagination. What is the dominant metaphor shaping our picture of discipleship?

Many words and metaphors are used to describe those who have accepted Jesus: disciple, follower, servant, friend, brother/sister, soldier. In different streams of the church, different metaphors dominate. For many in the evangelical tradition, the metaphor of the soldier has dominated, arising partly out of our nineteenth- and twentieth-century imperial history and our nation's success as a military power. Hymns like 'Onward Christian Soldiers' and 'Fight the Good Fight', as well as the description of the church as an army, are of course also triggered by New Testament imagery.

For some in our market-driven society perhaps another metaphor is gaining subconscious traction – that of God as the over-demanding boss who gives us too much to do, on too short a deadline, with not enough resources, and who will give us more when we've done that.

If, in our work-obsessed, market-driven culture, we have come to see God as a boss, then we will be heavily prone to living our lives under the burden of salvation by works. This is a danger in every age, but particularly in a culture like ours, which has made such a direct link between performance and significance.

Indeed, in contemporary Britain we have our own versions of a Pharisaic salvation by works: a legalistic obsession with ever-increasing levels of religious performance; consigning people to a never-ending treadmill of effort and failure, of guilt and shame, of ever-more obsessive ruminating on the tiniest of details; not doing great good for fear of breaking some minor man-made stipulation. Joyless legalism.

Take one example in contemporary Britain. Education. How we have foisted on our children an endless round of exams and performance measures! Your future depends on good SATs, 7A*s at GCSE, 4As at AS level, 3 As at A level and a 2:1 at university. How easy for our children to believe that their significance depends on their success, on their works. The same ideology pervades our workplaces: good works lead to significance; success leads to significance. This is the precise opposite of the gospel of grace by faith alone.

Dr Harold Rowdon, who taught church history at London Bible College (now London School of Theology), commented at his leaving address that evangelicals preach salvation by grace and faith alone, but live lives of salvation by works. It is never far away; it is at the heart of our culture.

Yes, Jesus is Lord, Jesus is Master. Yes, God is King of the universe, worthy of all honour, majesty and swift obedience. But what is the primary term that Jesus uses about God? It is not general; it is not boss. It is Father.

Time and again in the Gospel of John, this is how Jesus refers to God. In fact, there are 109 uses of the word 'father' in John's Gospel, and most of those involve Jesus referring to his Father. This is the primary way he sees God.

And in John 17:20–21 we have this amazing prayer:

> My prayer is not for them alone. I pray also for those who will believe in me through their message, that all of them may be one, Father, just as you are in me and I am in you. May they also be in us so that the world may believe that you have sent me.

May we have the same intimate relationship with the Father that Jesus does!

How do you picture yourself?

What if God is my heavenly Dad: how does that change my expectations of him? How does that change the way I see mission?

What does my heavenly Father want? Surely not that I exhaust myself in activism, that I am beset by guilt and try to assuage that guilt by involving myself in all kinds of activities? Surely not that I think the only thing that matters to him day by day is whether I've told someone verbally about his Son? We live every aspect of our lives for the honour of his name.

Remember, metaphors shape our imagination. So if the one who orders and shapes my life is *Abba*, what am I? We've seen that many words are used to describe those who have accepted Jesus – disciple, follower, servant, friend, brother/sister and soldier. But if we drill down a bit, we see that the primary metaphor that Jesus, Paul and John leave us with is sons and daughters.

When John writes about what those who have received Jesus can call themselves, he says, 'Yet to all who did receive him, to those who believed in his name, he gave the right to become children of God' (John 1:12). We don't have a right to health, wealth, marriage or a long life, but we do have a right to call ourselves the sons and daughters of God.

When Paul is writing to the Colossians, he tells the slaves in chapter 3:23–24 that they will have an inheritance from the Lord. Only sons inherited. He's telling slaves that they are sons!

In Galatians Paul writes to prevent the Christians drifting back into trying to earn their salvation by works. He tries to stop them believing that holiness consists in keeping laws, and so he reminds them of why God sent his Son:

> But when the set time had fully come, God sent his Son, born of a woman, born under the law, to redeem those under the law, that we might receive adoption to sonship. Because you are his sons, God sent the Spirit of his Son

into our hearts, the Spirit who calls out, 'Abba, Father.'
So you are no longer a slave, but God's child; and since
you are his child, God has made you also an heir.
(Galatians 4:4–7)

Why did God send his Son? So that we might be free, so
that we might be sons and daughters. It is not that *Abba*
does not have things for us to do. He gave his own Son the
immeasurably challenging task of giving his life for the sins
of all humankind. But it does mean that we can trust that
he is not driving us like some Pharaonic taskmaster to
make bricks without straw. He does not set before me
performance measures that are inappropriate to the
context I am in, the people I am with and the gifting he has
graced me with.

Because God is my Father, he is with me on my frontline.
Because God is my Father, when I ask for bread he will not
give me a scorpion. He will resource me.

Because God is my Father, he will turn all that happens
to me on my frontline to good. Because God is my Father,
it gives me confidence to see the frontline he has put me
on and the people he has put me with differently – as a gift,
a sacred trust.

Judith is a head teacher. She turned up at school on a
very cold February Monday to discover that the heating
had broken and several hundred children were about to
arrive. There was already plenty in her diary before the
boiler broke. But that's how her day began – figuring out
a way to get enough heaters in the classrooms to keep the

school open. Her day ended with a troublesome child who'd been troublesome rather too often before. And so, reluctantly, she found herself having to exclude him. Not the best of days on her frontline.

But when she got home, after what was really a grim day – when she might well have been justified in having a mega-whinge, or soothing herself with a glass or two of medicinal wine or a large tub of quadruple chocolate ice cream – something strange happened. As she put it, 'I found myself thanking God for trusting me with all that.'

God was trusting her, just as God had trusted Moses with the Israelites. These were the people God had given her to love. These were the challenges he was expecting her to handle – with him. And God is trusting us with our frontlines – trusting us with the people there, trusting us with the challenges there, trusting us with the tasks there, trusting us to be his people there. It's a privilege really, an honour.

We are sons and daughters of our heavenly Father, and the Father heart of God is the starting point for our evangelism on the frontline. Indeed, one of the things we've learned about helping people to be more intentional and fruitful in their evangelism is not to begin with dealing with all the fears that they might have or the difficult questions that someone might ask, but rather to begin with God.

God is the evangelist.
God wants people saved.
God is already on the job.
You have a part to play, however small.

So, begin by asking our heavenly Father if there is a particular person that he wants you to be concerned about, and participate with him in drawing them closer to him. And give thanks for your frontline – for the variety of ways you might be fruitful there for him; for the people he's given you to bless, care for and show and share the love of Christ with, in word and deed. And be confident in him – in the all-sufficient glory of his sacrifice for us on the cross; in his sovereign power to stretch out his hands to do might works; in the power of his Word to bring liberating truth; in the power of his Spirit to strengthen, guide and woo; in the truth that we do not go out into the world day by day as employees with a to-do list, but as precious sons and daughters of the King of kings. We are royalty, princes and princesses, sons and daughters, brothers and sisters of *Abba*, empowered to be faithful, freed to be free, transformed to be fruitful for him and to his glory. Amen.

Notes

1. Jim Collins, *Good to Great* (Random House, 2001).
2. Fred Kiel, *Return on Character* (Harvard Business Review Press, 2015).
3. London Institute of Contemporary Christianity (www.licc.org.uk).
4. See www.missionscotland.org.uk.

Whole-Life Worship

by Tim Chester

Tim Chester is pastor of Grace Church in Boroughbridge, North Yorkshire, and tutor with the Acts 29 Oak Hill Academy. He's the author of a number of books, including *From Creation to New Creation*, *Good News to the Poor*, *Delighting in the Trinity*, *You Can Change*, *A Meal with Jesus* and *1 Samuel for You*. His latest book, *Mission Matters: Love Says Go*, is part of the Keswick Ministries Foundations series. Tim is married with two daughters.

Whole-Life Worship: Psalm 18

I'll let you into a secret. I love wild swimming – swimming in rivers, lakes and the sea. I've had a few 'moments' doing it. A couple of years ago I was swimming in the sea in Scotland. I was tired. But when I put my feet down so I could rest, there was nothing there. I was out of my depth. So I started to swim to shore. But I was being moved back and forth in the swell. There was no strength in my limbs. I was starting to feel cold – which is a bad sign. I thought, 'This is serious. I could drown here.' Of course, I didn't shout for help because I'm a man!

Then finally, I put my feet down and felt solid ground. In that moment I knew I was safe. I was still in the water. It was still a struggle to reach the beach. But at any point I could put my feet down and feel solid rock.

My prayer is that something like that will happen this evening. Some of you may feel like the waves of life are overwhelming you. You may feel out of your depth. You may feel you're drowning under the pressures. It might be anxiety, loss, depression or guilt. Maybe you can't give it a name, but you're struggling to cope. You feel buffeted by the waves of life. I want you to put your feet down and feel firm ground underneath as you rest on God the Rock.

Turn with me to Psalm 18. Look at verses 4–5:

> The cords of death entangled me;
>> the torrents of destruction overwhelmed me.
> The cords of the grave coiled around me;
>> the snares of death confronted me.

These are the words of King David, Israel's greatest king. He lived about a thousand years before Jesus. David knows what it is to feel overwhelmed. The word 'grave' is 'Sheol', the word for the afterlife or hell. David feels like he's being destroyed, dragged down to hell. But David has learnt: 'The LORD is my rock, my fortress and my deliverer' (verse 2).

If you turn to the end of 2 Samuel, you'll find Psalm 18 repeated, almost word for word. This is the song David sings as he looks back on his life. So Psalm 18 shows how faith impacts the whole of our lives, in the sense of everything we do. But even more than that, this is worship that arises from seeing God at work throughout the whole of David's life. It gives us a way of making sense of our lives. Look at how the song opens in verses 1–2:

I love you, LORD, my strength.
The LORD is my rock, my fortress and my deliverer;
    my God is my rock, in whom I take refuge,
    my shield and the horn of my salvation, my stronghold.

The repeated word is 'my'. But this is not about David. David is saying, 'The LORD is everything to me. Throughout my life it's always been God who has protected me.'

In 2 Samuel this song is preceded and followed by a list of David's top soldiers, his 'mighty warriors' (23:8). When you read of their exploits, you realize they were hard men. Yet even with his mighty men, David's says in Psalm 18:17, often 'my foes . . . were too strong for me'. The mighty men are honoured. It is a bit like the acknowledgments page of a biography. David is saying, 'I wouldn't be where I am today without these men.' But the acknowledgment that really matters is: 'The LORD is my Rock.'

That's a kind of refrain to this song. Not only does it open the song, but it's repeated in the middle and towards the end:

For who is God besides the LORD?
    And who is the Rock except our God?
(verse 31)

The LORD lives! Praise be to my Rock!
    Exalted be my God my Saviour!
(verse 46)

'The LORD is my Rock.' What does this mean?

We worship God the Rock who is mighty to save (verses 1–19)

Look at verses 7–13: When God came, 'the earth trembled . . . mountains shook . . . smoke rose . . . He parted the heavens and came down [in] dark clouds . . . The LORD thundered from heaven.'

This is the language of Mount Sinai. God rescued his people from slavery in Egypt and met with them at Mount Sinai. This is how it's described in Exodus 19: 'There was thunder and lightning, with a thick cloud over the mountain . . . Mount Sinai was covered with smoke, because the LORD descended on it in fire . . . the whole mountain trembled violently' (Exodus 19:16, 18). Then look what happens in verses 15–16 of the psalm:

> The valleys of the sea were exposed . . .
>> at the blast of breath from your nostrils . . .
>> he drew me out of deep waters.

This is God parting the Red Sea to deliver his people (Exodus 14).

David is describing the exodus in these verses. He's not exaggerating for effect. He is describing something that really happened in history – the exodus from Egypt, the encounter at Sinai, the parting of the Red Sea.

Except that it wasn't something that happened to David – not in the sense that he was there at the time. He was born several centuries later. But in a very real sense it *did* happen to him. It happened *for* him. The freedom he enjoys, his relationship with God, his identity as God's king – all are founded on the exodus. That was the moment when God liberated Israel and made them his people. In that moment at the Red Sea, David was drawn out of the waters because Israel was drawn out of the waters (verse 16). He was rescued from his enemies (verse 17) and brought into a spacious place (verse 19). He lives in Palestine because of that moment. And every deliverance David experienced – and there were many – was based on that great deliverance.

David is saying, 'Whenever I felt overwhelmed by life or entangled by death, I would look back to the exodus. I would confront my *feelings* with the *fact* of the exodus. God has created his people and he will not abandon his promises.'

It is exactly the same for us – except that we can look back to the resurrection of Jesus. After all, that's what the exodus was pointing to. This is a psalm of resurrection. Jesus was overwhelmed by death, as verse 4 describes. The cords of hell coiled around him, as verse 5 describes. But God reached down to lift him up from death (verse 16).

And this is our experience – if we are in Christ by faith. God has intervened in our lives with resurrection power (Romans 6:3–5). So you can say, as David could, 'Whenever I feel overwhelmed by life or entangled by death, I can look to the resurrection of Jesus. I can confront my *feelings* with the *fact* of the resurrection. That's the sign that God will recreate his people and will not abandon his promises.'

David himself didn't feel the earth shake at Mount Sinai. He didn't hear the thunder, see the lightning or smell the smoke. But he realized that his experiences were an echo of Sinai. David didn't just get lucky with his slingshot when he faced Goliath; God intervened on his behalf. David didn't just get lucky when he escaped Saul; God intervened on his behalf.

And when God intervenes in your life, it might simply involve the help of another Christian, a timely 'coincidence' or a message at Keswick. But David wants us to recognize that these things are acts of the earth-shaking, fire-breathing, darkness-dispelling God.

Let your imagination run riot! The next coincidence, the next illness cured by a doctor, the next timely word from a friend – see behind these things the God of the exodus and the God of resurrection. This is how to read history. This is how to understand your life.

- Next time you want to say, 'I was struck by something when I read in my Bible', instead say, 'Jesus spoke to me through his Word.'
- Instead of saying, 'A weird thing happened to me today', say, 'The Father reached down into my life to provide a great opportunity for me . . .'
- Instead of saying, 'I don't know how I got through it', say, 'The Spirit helped me with resurrection power.'

My friend Matt's daughter has brain cancer. Last week he said, 'I wanted to rip the soap dispenser off the wall and smash it up. I don't know what stopped me.' And I could say, 'I do know: it was the Holy Spirit helping you with resurrection power.'

We worship God the Rock who makes *us* mighty to serve (verses 30–49)

The second half of the psalm is about how God made David mighty to rule. It starts in verses 30–31 with another reference to God as our Rock. Then run your eyes over verses 32–45. David is armed with strength. His feet do not give way. He crushes his enemies. Why? Because of God. 'It is God who arms me with strength' (verse 32).

'Your help has made me great,' says David in verse 35. David is not a self-made man. He didn't pull himself out of obscurity. It's God who has made him great. Look at verse 27: 'You save the humble, but bring low those whose eyes are haughty [literally *high*].' Or verse 48: 'You exalted me above my foes.' 'Haughty' in verse 27 and 'exalted' in verse 48 are the same word. God has brought down 'the high' and lifted David 'high'.

When we are first introduced to King Saul in 1 Samuel, we're told that he was taller than anyone else (1 Samuel 10:23). When we first meet David, we're told he was the 'youngest', literally 'the smallest' (1 Samuel 16:11). But now the high one has been brought low, and little David has been raised high in his place. Not only has God made David king of Israel, he also says that God has 'made me the head of nations', for God 'subdues nations under me' (Psalm 18:43, 47).

As far as I'm aware, none of us is a king. As the final verse hints, this psalm is fulfilled in Jesus, God's anointed, David's great descendant. Just like David, Jesus humbled himself and God exalted him, giving him the name that is above every name (Philippians 2:8–9). Jesus is the King of God's people and the King of the nations.

So in one sense this psalm is not about you. It's about Christ. But if you're *in* Christ and *with* Christ, then you share his authority. This psalm is being fulfilled today through the mission of the church. The kingdom of Christ is extended as we proclaim the word of Christ. Through our evangelism, Christ is being made 'the head of nations' (Revelation 2:26–27).

How will we do that? How will we face hostility? We've talked this week about whole-life discipleship. How are you going to live for Christ in a hostile workplace? In a troubled home? What are the troubles to which you'll be returning? Think of David: living as an outlaw, in the heat of battle, his family torn apart, deposed by his own son. Verse 32 says, 'It is God who arms me with strength and keeps my way secure.'

God doesn't just call you to serve him. He also *empowers* you to serve him. *God gives all you need, to do all he asks.* The LORD our Rock arms you, keeps you, trains you, helps you, provides for you, strengthens you, delivers you – that's all language from this psalm. So we say,

> The LORD lives! Praise be to my Rock!
>   Exalted be God, my Saviour!
> (verse 46)

We worship God the Rock who makes us righteous in Christ (verses 20–29)

The first half of this song describes how God is mighty to save. The second half describes how God makes us mighty to serve. The centre is verses 20–29. Let me give you a flavour. Look at verse 20: 'The LORD has dealt with me according to my righteousness.' Or verse 24: 'The LORD has rewarded me according to my righteousness.'

At this point you might be saying, 'Hang on a minute. Isn't this the David who committed adultery and murder? If David is rewarded according to his righteousness, then surely he's in big trouble! How can he say this?' God 'saves me from my enemies,' says David in verse 48. But what if God is your enemy?

Part of the answer is that David is declaring his covenant faithfulness. He is righteous in the same way Abraham believed and it was *credited* to him as righteousness. (Paul connects Abraham and David in this way in Romans 4.) David isn't claiming to be sinless, but to have a right standing within the covenant, a covenant that included provision for sin through sacrifice. After David's adultery, the prophet Nathan says, 'The LORD has taken away your sin. You are not going to die' (2 Samuel 12:13).

So God blesses David because he overlooks David's sins. But how can God do this?

The answer brings us back to the refrain of the song: the LORD is my Rock. Something of what that means is self-evident: God is firm, reliable and solid. We can depend on him. He provides a foundation for our lives (Matthew 7:24–27). But two stories show us why David makes *this* the refrain of his song and – since David is looking back in this song – the refrain of his whole life. These two stories show why 'the LORD is my Rock' was the soundtrack of David's life.

Story 1: In 1 Samuel 23 King Saul is trying to kill David. Saul is going along one side of a mountain; David is hurrying on the other side. It seems a bit like Tom and Jerry – backwards and forwards. Then the Philistines attack and Saul has to abandon the chase. That mountain is simply referred to as 'the rock' (1 Samuel 23:25). David is protected by 'the rock'. The rock comes between him and Saul. It becomes known as 'the Rock of Parting', because it keeps David apart from his enemies.

Now at the end of his life David says in verse 31, 'Who is the Rock?' 'The LORD is my Rock.' All along God has been like that rock mountain. God stands between us and our enemies. As death approaches, as judgment approaches, God himself interposes in the person of his Son. Jesus stands between us and our enemies. He absorbs the full force of divine wrath. As a result, he becomes 'my rock, my fortress and my deliverer' (verse 2).

Story 2: David is not the first person in the Bible to call God 'the Rock'. Moses also sang a song as he reflected at the end of his life. And what is its refrain? 'God is my Rock.' He mentions it six times (Deuteronomy 32:4, 15, 18, 30, 31, 36–37). This reflects a defining moment in the life of Moses. Soon after God has rescued Israel out of slavery, the people complain. They're testing God – putting him on trial. What will God do?

The choreography is very significant. The Israelites have put God on trial through their grumbling. And so God arranges a courtroom. The representatives of Israel are on one side (Exodus 17:5), and God is on the other side. He says, 'I will stand there before you by the rock at Horeb' (verse 6). This is the case of 'Israel vs. God'. In the middle is Moses with his staff, and God specifically says that this is the staff that brought judgment on Egypt (verse 5). So Moses is, as it were, the judge. All this takes place 'in front of the people', so everyone can see what happens (verse 5).

We know that the Israelites are guilty and deserve to be condemned. We know that God is innocent and deserves to be vindicated. But God tells Moses, 'Strike the rock' (verse 6). Moses brings down the rod of judgment *on God*. God takes the judgment that his people deserve. As a result, blessing flows to the people. In this case it literally flows, for water comes out from the rock to quench the people's thirst (verse 6).

Paul explains that the rock was Christ: 'they drank from the spiritual rock that accompanied them, and that rock was Christ' (1 Corinthians 10:4). The story was a picture of, and pointer to, the cross. At the cross the great court case between God and humanity comes to its climax. On one side is guilty humanity – you and I – deserving con-demnation. On the other side is the perfect, sinless Son of God, Christ the Rock. And God the Father says, 'Strike the rock.' The rod of his judgment falls on Jesus. So when

Moses calls God 'the Rock' and when David calls God 'the Rock', they mean he is the Rock who takes our judgment on himself.

This psalm is not a challenge to achieve. Christ has achieved everything for us. David's message to us is this: 'There is a Rock on which you can stand. If you put your feet on that Rock, then you can keep your head above water.'

Stop swimming. Take a moment to put your feet down. Feel solid ground underneath. God has dealt with your sin. And he will bring you safely to the shore. When you leave this tent, you will still be in the water and the waves will still buffet you. But there is a Rock beneath your feet. Stretch your feet out – stretch your faith out – and feel it there. Stop trying to be your own saviour. Discover afresh that Christ is 'my rock, my fortress and my deliverer'.

Whole-Life Purpose

by Vanessa Conant

Vanessa Conant is Team Rector at St Mary's, Walthamstow. She began her career at a church in the outer estates of West London, and then worked as a fundraiser for Christian Aid and Crisis, before becoming Associate Rector at St Paul's and St George's Church, Edinburgh. Her passions are for food, film, sunshine, exploring new places, history, teaching the Bible in new ways, building community, encouraging people to explore their vocation and developing young leaders.

Whole-Life Purpose: Jeremiah 29

The writer Mark Twain said that the two most important days in our life are the day when we are born, and the day when we find out why. We long for meaning and for purpose. We need it like our bodies need food. It is the thing that gives life, hope and future hope to us. I read recently that every month half a million people google the phrase 'the meaning of life'. So desperate are we, so deeply do we need to know: Why are we here? What is the purpose of our lives? How can we live well in this world? And tonight we have the response to that question through the lens of Jeremiah 29.

I have to say that these verses are more familiar to me than other parts of Jeremiah, perhaps because years ago someone gave me a mug with 'You know the plans I have for you' written on it. And on lots of different occasions

I've been given a greetings card with those same words on it. The danger for me– maybe you're not as guilty of this as I am – is that I reduce those words a little bit. They become a slogan or a twee platitude. They can be like a guardian angel God, there to comfort and reassure me that the plans God has are good.

Actually, this is a deeply challenging and provocative text. Jeremiah 29 is written into a really difficult situation, not warning people of impending trouble, but written to people for whom the worst has already happened. They are in the deepest trouble – dislocated, cut off, far away from everything that matters and is precious to them. And into that situation come words about how their purpose and God's purposes are aligned; how they might find their purpose through God's purpose. We are looking at deeply challenging, surprising, unexpected words. Words that ask us to take a different perspective; words that ask us to look at the world with paradoxes in it; words that ask us to see things differently. So, join with me in travelling through this letter from Jeremiah and looking at how we might find purpose for our whole life, how we might live that whole-life purpose, and how we might join up our purpose with the purposes of God.

Face the truth with courage

The first invitation I see in this text is to find our whole-life purpose by facing the truth with courage. Jeremiah 29 is really a response to the chapters that have gone before.

You may pick up in the text that Jeremiah is responding to false prophets who have been proclaiming to the people of Israel the very palatable words that this painful exile in Babylon will last only two years. Well, who doesn't want to believe that? Everyone wants to believe Hananiah the prophet, because it's much more appealing to believe that your suffering will come to an end.

I don't know if you remember when the economic crisis first happened. There were plenty of people saying, 'This is just a blip, this is just a bubble!' Or when we've entered into military conflict and leaders have said, 'It'll be over in months – ten months and we'll be done!' It's easy to believe, because it's a more palatable truth. But into that false comfort, into that dishonest reassurance, Jeremiah – he who caused conflict and hostility – speaks words that once again no-one wants to hear. Who wants to be with Jeremiah at a dinner party? Not me! But the words he speaks are truth, words of searing honesty. They are the deep call of Yahweh to his people to come and discover their true vocation in God, to return again to God, to face the truth with courage.

Jeremiah is saying to the people of Israel, and us, that our whole-life purpose, our future hope, the ordering of our steps, the living well in the place where we find ourselves, is not to be found by pretending that the world is other than it is. Our purpose is not found by believing in something that sounds affirming, but is actually inaccurate. It's not found by living in denial or retreating from reality. Our whole-life purpose is found by facing the truth of what stands before us, with courage and determination.

I think there are two parts of Jeremiah's call. First, there is the call to find our purpose by being transformed by faith in the one true God. The second part is to be people who transform the world around us by our faith in the one true God. This is what the Lord says: 'When seventy years are completed for Babylon, I will come to you' (verse 10). Jeremiah wants the people of Israel to know that the land which is the source of their identity, confidence and hope – the land that is so significant and imbued with meaning – is lost. And it's not lost briefly or temporarily, not for two years as Hananiah says; it is deeply, profoundly lost for generations. Jeremiah wants them to face that truth, because in facing that truth, they will find their new vocation. To accept that loss is to put their faith in God who is leading them into new life.

This episode in Israel's history foreshadows the gospel of Jesus Christ. The exile is a death that the people of Israel must encounter. What will come after it? If they are willing to embrace that landlessness and loss, there is new life. Here is the promise of truth that radical loss leads to newness of life. This is an upside-down kingdom. This is the world of the Beatitudes. This is Easter Sunday and Good Friday. This is the truth that loss and the acceptance of loss, facing the truth with courage, leads profoundly to a new vocation, new life, new faith for the people of Israel.

Christians in this country find themselves at the margins too. We find a church that is waning in influence, diminishing in power. Sometimes the temptation is to stay in our places of grief, recognizing that place of exile for us as the people of God is no longer at the centre, but at the edge. Or sometimes the desire within me is to deny it and say, 'It's just a blip; it won't last.' But I wonder if there is a call to the exiles, echoing here to us today, to face truth with courage. A call to face this situation of loss, knowing that to embrace it might be the way of resurrection, new faith and new life. How might we be transformed by facing the truth with courage? That's the first part of the call to purpose in facing the truth.

What about the second part: to transform the world around us? I remember a couple of years ago watching an American lawyer named Bryan Stevenson speak. He campaigns for equal access to justice around the United States. He tells a story about Ms Carr, an elderly woman in Montgomery, Alabama, who used to invite him over occasionally for afternoon tea. And one time Ms Carr invited her friend to join them for tea. Her friend just happened to be the great civil rights campaigner Rosa Parks, the woman who initiated the Montgomery bus boycotts. And Ms Carr invited Bryan for tea and said, 'You just listen, boy. You just listen to what we are going to say in our conversations', and so he did. And at the end of their conversation Rosa Parks turned to him and said, 'What are you doing with your life? What are you hoping will happen?' And Bryan said, 'Well, Ms Parks, I am trying to campaign for equal access to the justice system in America. I'm trying to reduce the number of young black men who are incarcerated in prison. I am trying to stop children being put into prison. I am trying to find new ways to deal with offending. I am trying to stop the death penalty.' And on and on he went with all his hopes and plans. Rosa Parks paused and looked at him, and then she said, 'Boy, you're going to be tired, tired, tired. You are going to need to be brave, brave, brave.'

This is the call to the Israelites living in exile: to live another way, to live the purposes of God, they need to be brave, brave, brave. They live in a land where they are not in power. They are at the margins and they have very little opportunity to speak to power. The call of Yahweh is to face that truth with courage and to live with integrity and wellness. And so it is for us: our purpose is to live, whether at the margins or in the centre, with courage, and to be brave in that. We live in a land that is governed by other values. We live in a land that says what matters is the market, what matters in the growing economy, and so the rich get richer, and the poor get poorer. To speak into this situation we need to be brave, brave, brave.

We live in a time when climate change is happening and we will all be affected by the challenges of the environment. And we need to think about how we as Christians will respond to that, unselfishly, sacrificially, with our eyes on those who have the least, who are most affected. We need to be brave, brave, brave. And we live in a time in which the world is ravaged by war and violence, and where Christians in the Middle East are facing almost utter annihilation. How will we respond? We need to be brave, brave, brave. Whole-life purpose will not come from us pretending that things are other than they are. It won't come from denying it, or hiding or retreating or finding safety in a false reality. We have to hear the call of Jeremiah to discover our true vocation. We must face that radical loss knowing it is the way of resurrection, knowing it is the way of new life. And we have to be courageous and brave to speak the values of the kingdom in a foreign land.

Join in the wider purposes of God

The second invitation is this: whole-life purpose comes when we join in with the wider purposes of God. In this exile, in the midst of pain, hopelessness, loss and disorientation, somewhere here are the wider purposes of God. And the invitation to the people of Israel is not to decide their own purpose, but somehow to join in with the wider purposes of God.

The former Archbishop of Canterbury, Rowan Williams, said, 'Mission is finding out what God is doing, and joining in.' That's really the invitation to the Israelites and to us: What is God doing? How can I join in? And because God is love, we can be sure that the purposes of God are love. So the invitation to the Israelites is not just to find what God is doing, but to find what the purposes and the way of love is. Find out what it means to live with love in the place to which he calls them. In their case, it means settle there. Jeremiah instructs them to build communities, marry, have sons and daughters, have relationships with one another, and find love and stability there. The purposes of God invite us in to discern what it means to live in the place where we are called. What does it mean to be people of love in the situation where we find ourselves? What does it mean for you? What does it mean to live well and join in with the purposes of God?

There is also this call not just to trust the wider purposes of God, but to put hope in them. The Israelites are wrenched from their centre of worship, they find themselves lost, far away from the temple, far away from what was familiar to them, and something is transformed in their whole community by the process of being in exile. Being in exile means that they begin to pray differently; they begin to seek God with a purity of heart that they haven't had before; and they begin to discover a commitment to live in his ways. God says in verses 12–13,

> Then you will call on me and come and pray to me, and I will listen to you. You will seek me and find me when you seek me with all your heart.

There is this sense in which the Israelites are learning in exile what they couldn't seem to learn while they were in Jerusalem. They have this opportunity to return to God in a new and deep way. These are the people, with their sons and daughters, who will return from exile, flawed and full of error, desperate to restore the kingdom, desperate to restore the temple, desperate to worship God, desperate to point to the glory of God.

Somehow, when we join in with the wider purposes of God, we get to see a far bigger picture, a far wider agenda.

We get to discover the deeper truths of who God is. In the place where God has called you, as you face the truth with courage, as you seek to transform the world around you, how might you discern the wider purposes of God? And will you trust, will you have hope, that these purposes are purposes of love; purposes that will point to the glory of God; purposes that will point to another kingdom.

Seek the prosperity of the city

The final invitation in Jeremiah 29 is that whole-life purpose comes by seeking the prosperity of the city. Verse 7 says,

> Seek the peace and prosperity of the city to which I have carried you into exile. Pray to the LORD for it, because if it prospers, you too will prosper.

Yet again, Jeremiah is giving a new purpose and a new vocation to the people of Israel, which is to 'seek the prosperity of the city' – or in some translations, 'the welfare of the city' – into which they are carried. This is utterly scandalous. Jeremiah is telling the Israelites not just to seek economic well-being, but actually to seek the *shalom*, the wholeness, the healing, the well-being, the peace – not just of your neighbours, your friends and your communities, but of the very people who have taken you into captivity and ripped from you what you love. 'Love your enemies and pray for those who persecute you' (Matthew 5:44). The gospel whispers through Jeremiah again.

Jeremiah is not saying that God condones persecution or that he had intended this oppression all along. Jeremiah is saying that by living well with integrity and generosity, by seeking the well-being of the land, the Israelites point to another kingdom at work. They say, 'This is not all there is, this is not the ending; we wait for fulfilment, we wait for something more.' Exile is not the whole story. While you find yourself on the margins, how will you live well by the values of another kingdom?

And more than seeking the well-being and healing of the city, the Israelites were to seek the common good, because in its well-being was their well-being. As one writer has put it, 'This invitation to seek, above all, the common good, is so challenging for us. It means we pursue justice in our community, we look for compassion wherever we can find it, and we reject violence and inequality.' And we do that not just for those whom we love and those who are around us, but for those who might oppose us, for those we find difficult, for those who have been challenging or hurtful. We seek their well-being because in their well-being is our well-being. This is the deep human call coming from God: that my well-being is inextricably bound up in yours. Those two things cannot be separated, and to find purpose is to live in that truth. And so, we have food banks, street pastors, night shelters, meals for and with homeless people, youth projects, children's work, debt centres and credit unions. The call is to campaign for refugees, asylum seekers and trafficked slaves, and not to let the poor be rejected, demonized or forgotten. Pray faithfully for the welfare of your village, town or city, day after day after day after day, knowing that in their welfare is your welfare. This is our call; this is the call to find purpose in pursuing the common good.

For the Israelites, the point was not to pursue these things so that they got back everything they had lost. The point was to bear witness to a God who was good, to a God whose power is greater, to a God whose love is greater. And for us too, the idea is not that we send ourselves into a whirlwind of frenzied charitable activity, but that we follow in the way of Daniel, Esther and Joseph, and invest in the places around us, while maintaining obedience and faithfulness in the God who calls us.

One theologian has translated 'seek the welfare of the city' as 'seek the salvation of the culture to which I sent you'. And what he means is: when we live this way – when we find our purpose in pursuing the common good, when we put the welfare of others first, when we go beyond our comfort zones and beyond our fears – we are bearing witness to the saving love, mercy and grace of Jesus Christ. Our purpose is to be found in revealing him to others.

At the end of this passage, in verse 14, there are words of comfort and hope:

> 'I will be found by you,' declares the LORD, 'and will bring you back from captivity. I will gather you from all the nations and places where I have banished you,' declares the LORD, 'and will bring you back to the place from which I carried you into exile.'

There is reassurance here in God's words: deep reassurance for the people of Israel, that to live this way and to face the truth with courage, to join their purposes in with God's, to seek the common good, will lead in the end to their deep *shalom*, and to the return of all that is hopeful for them. And for us, there is deeper reassurance still – Jesus Christ, who died and rose again for us, will strengthen and equip us to live this way. We don't have to do these things in our own strength or in our own power; he will equip and guide us. He will equip us to face the truth with courage, to discern the ways of love and how we can be part of them, and to seek the welfare of the places where we live, knowing that there is no other way to find healing and wholeness.

Radical Integrity

by *Malcolm Duncan*

Revd Malcolm Duncan is the leader of Gold Hill Baptist Church in Buckinghamshire, and Chair of the Spring Harvest Planning Group. Malcolm is passionate about the importance of Christians being 'good news people' and about the importance of preaching, service, advocacy, prayer and partnership so that followers of Jesus can be effective in changing the world. He is also the founder and chair of the Catalyst Network, a network of churches across the UK and beyond that is committed to encountering God and engaging with society. Malcolm is married to Debbie and they have four children.

Radical Integrity: 1 Thessalonians 2:1–12

One of the great challenges of living today as a follower of Jesus is how to live faithfully for him. And if we are not careful, we can fall into one of two traps: we will either let the culture shape the way we live out our calling to be followers of Jesus Christ, or we will allow church traditions, which may be more important to us than the actual truth of the gospel, to become shackles that bind us. We have to be careful to avoid both.

The greatest danger to the church today in the United Kingdom and Europe is not radicalized Islam or aggressive secularism. The greatest danger is an apathetic church: a community of Jesus' followers who have lost confidence in the gospel, in the Word of God and in God's purposes for the world. But when we read of Paul writing to the Thessalonians, we are confronted by someone who is radical in his faithfulness to God and to the gospel, and in the way that he lives out his life.

I want to unpack 1 Thessalonians 2:1–12 with you this evening to see if God can teach us anything about what it means to be radical in our integrity. What was at the heart of Paul's life that made him relentlessly faithful to God? What was it about his understanding of himself, God, the church and its place in the world that meant he was never dominated by the circumstances around him and he never compromised his faithfulness to the gospel?

Engaging with culture

I want to explore just five key areas from the passage. First, I want to unpack how Paul's integrity shone through in the way he engaged with his culture. In verses 1–2 Paul says that when he proclaimed the gospel in Philippi, there was a great deal of trouble. In Acts 17 we read the story of him being thrown into prison because of his faithfulness to the gospel. Wherever he went, there was either a revival or a riot. Whether he went to Ephesus, Philippi, Lystra or Thessalonica, there was a response to the gospel that he proclaimed.

But here is the interesting thing about the apostle Paul: when he engaged with the culture around him, he avoided relativizing the gospel. He did, however, contextualize the gospel – there is a difference between these two ideas. To relativize the gospel is to wrap it up and put it in the culture. To contextualize the gospel is to understand the tenants at the heart of the gospel and to make sure they connect with the culture around us, without changing the gospel. Paul refused to relativize the gospel, but instead he contextualized it.

One of the great examples of this is his engagement with those who were seeking the 'unknown God' at Mars Hill. If we were chatting with a group of people we didn't know, but who had some kind of understanding of the 'unknown God', many of us would begin by saying to them, 'You are wrong about this! Here are the three points that you have to understand about this altar.' Paul didn't start there. Instead, he said, 'I see you have an altar here; you are seeking truth. Let me begin where you are and take you on a journey so that you can see what the truth really is.' What he didn't do was change the gospel or change his message fundamentally to fit the culture.

I'm aware that what I am about to say might be controversial. The biggest challenge that we face over the next twenty years as Christians is what we do with the Bible. The issue of same-sex marriage, how we engage with society, how we conduct ourselves as Christians, all hangs upon how we handle the Bible. And the fundamental challenge for us is: do we believe that the Scriptures speak the true Word of God and that therefore they have the power to transform the culture? Or do we believe that the culture will transform the Bible? I pray that we are believers who understand that the Bible does not sit under the culture, being changed and altered by it, but instead the Bible transforms the culture.

Paul had a radical integrity, because at the core of who he was there was an unchanging and unwavering commitment to God and his purposes for the world. In the 1960s that great Welsh preacher, Martyn Lloyd-Jones, explained that the church will be most effective in the world when we are most different from the world, even if we are hated for a while. It isn't our job to fit into the culture. It is not our job to change the core of who we are in order to be more popular.

Let me tell you something that might surprise you. No denomination, Christian charity or individual church that has liberalized its doctrine on the person and work of Jesus Christ or the authority of the Bible has grown. For one generation they get a little bigger, but the second and third generation after that are depleted of numbers, resources, energy and vision. Why? Because at the heart of who we are is this radical call to be followers of Jesus Christ, to lay down our lives for him, to do what he wants, to go where he calls us. And Paul approached this issue knowing that to be true.

As Christians, we can often think that society should applaud us, welcome us, embrace us, and that it is abnormal for the church to be given a hard time. It is not abnormal for the church to be challenged, persecuted, mocked or ridiculed. It is normal – that is what we are told to expect in the New Testament. Paul says here in verse 2, '. . . but with the help of our God we dared to tell you his gospel in the face of strong opposition'. Will we do the same thing? Will you dare to be faithful to God, in work, in the face of strong opposition? Will you as a local church dare to be faithful to God in the face of strong opposition? Will you act with integrity? Will you live out what you believe, not expecting the culture to embrace you, but instead recognizing that it is highly likely that it won't.

You and I have a choice: we can act with radical integrity and be faithful to what God has called us to be, or we can be absorbed into our culture. If we are absorbed into our culture, then within a generation we will have lost our effectiveness as the body of Christ and our witness in the world. You might say, 'But the Bible says that Jesus has promised to build his church and that the gates of hell will not prevail against it!' (see Matthew 16:18). Do not read that to mean that the church will always be a powerful witness in this nation. Look at the church in North Africa and the Middle East – it is still there, but it was once much stronger, more powerful, and much clearer in its witness to Jesus Christ. There are still many churches in those nations, but they have shrunk. There is no guarantee whatsoever that the church in Britain will grow and grow. In fact, I have a hunch that we will see the church diminish in size but grow in effectiveness, as we discover what it means to be a faithful group of people who stand up in the culture for Christ.

Understanding the content of the message

The second issue we need to grapple with if we are to be radically faithful in our integrity is the idea of the content of what Paul said. Did you notice something in the passage that we heard again and again? Look at verse 2: 'but with the help of our God we dared to tell you his gospel.' Did you notice that? *His* gospel. You could translate it 'the gospel of God'. In verse 4 Paul talks about being entrusted with the gospel, and in verse 13 he speaks twice about the power of the Word of God. In verses 8 and 9 he talks about the gospel of God. For Paul, there is an idea behind the gospel which is not allowed to be changed. He is radically faithful because he understands the gospel to be something that he is entrusted with.

Another challenge we are facing in European and North American Christianity is that we are confused about the gospel. We either think it is ours, in the sense that we own it, or we redefine it to make it sound like God calls us just to be nice people – that is not the gospel! Or we understand that the gospel means that we just do nice things in the world and that God does everything else – that is not the gospel either. Be careful that you do not confuse two terms in your understanding of God's purposes in the world – one is gospel and the other is mission.

God's mission in the world is to transform it – hook, line and sinker. There will come a day where every aspect of the created order is transformed. A day when sorrow, suffering, sickness and death will be no more. That moment will be initiated at a specific point in time and in history when the Lord Jesus Christ returns, the clouds break, the trumpet sounds and the voice of the archangel announces that God has returned in the form of Jesus Christ. In that moment, the world will be transformed – hallelujah!

But we must be careful that we don't confuse God's mission in the world with the good news, the gospel, of Jesus Christ. Here is the gospel – I don't need to guess what it is; I don't need to try to work it out. The apostle Paul tells us in 1 Corinthians 15:3–5 that

> Christ died for our sins according to the Scriptures, that he was buried, that he was raised on the third day according to the Scriptures, and that he appeared to Cephas, and then to the Twelve.

He goes on to explain that Jesus also appeared to him and to 500 others. This is the good news. You and I, brothers and sisters, are not free to change that gospel. It is a baton that has been handed to us, and that we must then hand on to the generation that comes after us. We cannot dilute it or turn it into something else. Why? Because only that message has the power to break the power of sin; only that message is able to transform broken lives; only that message has the power to give hope to hopeless people; only that message has the power to conquer death. No other message! We are not called just to be nice people. We are not called just to make a difference; we are called to make disciples. We are called to point people back to this glorious good news that God was in Christ reconciling the world to himself.

When Paul wrote to almost anybody in the New Testament, he talked about his confidence in the gospel (see Romans 1:16). We too can be confident that this gospel works! When we proclaim the gospel – that Christ died for our sins according to the Scriptures, was buried and rose again – when we offer people that message of life, their lives are utterly transformed. That is why wherever Paul went there was a revival or a riot, because he proclaimed the lordship of Jesus. All of the gospel sermons, all of the sermons in the book of Acts, explained that Jesus died and was resurrected, and that God had now proclaimed him Lord.

You will never see a gospel message in the New Testament that says, 'Jesus is Lord if you want him to be'; 'Jesus is Lord if you ask him to be' – that is not how any of the apostles preached the good news. Here is what they preached: that God was in Christ transforming the world; that he was murdered as a result of sin; that he was buried and three days later God raised him from the dead, and in so doing conquered sin, death and hell; and God the Father has now proclaimed him as Lord of all creation. Jesus is Lord – that is good news! And when we proclaim that and invite people to respond to that, we see change in their hearts and lives. Paul's radical faithfulness, his integrity, was built on a willingness not to back away from what the gospel meant, not to back away from the fact that the culture would reject him.

Understanding your commission

Thirdly, Paul understood that he was commissioned by God:

For the appeal we make does not spring from error or impure motives, nor are we trying to trick you. On the contrary, we speak as those approved by God to be entrusted with the gospel. We are not trying to please people but God, who tests our hearts. You know we never used flattery, nor did we put on a mask to cover up greed – God is our witness. We were not looking for praise from people, not from you or anyone else, even though as apostles of Christ we could have asserted our authority. Instead, we were like young children among you.

(verses 3–7)

Paul understood that God had called him, commissioned him, and his life was now about pleasing him. So Paul refused to meddle in error, impure motives or misunderstanding. He didn't want to make money, he wasn't about persuading people unfairly, he wasn't going to tell them a lie, he wasn't going to water the message down and he wasn't going to tell them an untruth. He wasn't motivated by his own personality. He didn't care what people thought of him, because he was commissioned by God to proclaim this gospel message.

And we too are called by God. When all is said and done, we live out our lives before an audience of one. So don't listen to people who tell you that you are never going to be able to do it. Don't let other people's anxieties or apprehensions make you give up on what God has called you to be. Don't allow yourself to lower the standard of the gospel just to be popular. Don't turn the gospel into something you make money out of. Don't turn church into something that is no more than a glorified social club. Instead, have confidence in the fact that when God calls us, he equips us and enables us to live for him.

In verse 10 Paul says he has behaved in a holy and blameless way, encouraging the believers in Thessalonica, comforting them and urging them to keep going, because he knew who he was in God and he knew what God had asked him to do. He uses a number of lovely little images to help them understand that. He says that he didn't try to manipulate them: 'Instead, we were like young children among you' (verse 7). This is a picture of innocence and trust. Then he switches to three other pictures. He says he was like a nursing mother caring for them. The language he uses is tender, gentle and kind. Next, he addresses them as brothers and sisters, bringing an equality into his relationship with them. He says, 'I could have lorded it over you. I could have behaved as if I was a very important person and that you had to listen to me. But I chose not to do that. Instead, I chose to act out of integrity and behave with confidence in God's calling upon my life, his promise to provide for me and with a humbleness that means I am willing to talk to you as equals.' And yet he also uses the image of a father, as he challenges, guides and helps the believers to understand how they are to live for God in the world in which they find themselves.

Understanding the community of faith

The fourth thing that I wanted to pick up is this idea of Paul understanding what the community of faith was supposed to be. In chapter 1:1 he talks to the church in Thessalonica and addresses them in 'God the Father and the Lord Jesus Christ'. In 1:3 he commends them for their work of faith, labour of love and evidence of hope. In verse 4 he says he knows that they are chosen by God. Then in chapter 2:14 he talks about them being God's church, and their identity being in Christ Jesus. Be careful, brothers and sisters, that you don't turn the church into something else. Before we are anything, a church is a group of people centred on the Lord Jesus Christ. He is the one who demands our allegiance; he is the one who has rescued us. We remain faithful to him, even if the world laughs at us and tells us we are wrong. The church is primarily a group of people who have experienced the rescuing, redeeming work of God.

'Are you saying, Malcolm, that everybody in the church must be born again?' Well, yes, everybody in the church invisible, the true church. Then there is a wider community of people who are travelling towards God, and we must work out a way of embracing them, walking with them and treating them with respect, dignity and love. But never confuse the two. The only thing that gains you entry into the family of God is being born again by the Holy Spirit, responding to God as he has revealed himself to us in Jesus Christ. Nothing else gains you entry to the church. Singing in the choir or reading the Bible doesn't make you a Christian. Keith Green once said that going to the library doesn't make you a book, so going to church doesn't make you a Christian! The only thing that makes you part of that family of faith is having been regenerated by the power of the Holy Spirit after you have confessed the lordship of Jesus.

Understanding the consequences of living for Christ

This brings me to my final point: the consequences of this radical integrity. In verse 14 and following, Paul tells the Thessalonians that they are going to suffer and go through hardships for what they believe in. If you want to follow Jesus, you are going to be persecuted (2 Timothy 2:10). If you want to stand up for Christ, Britain will not applaud you. Your community is not going to say, 'Thank goodness for you!' You will have a hard time, so we need to change our expectations.

Paul's radical integrity could be summed up by this simple idea: at his core, he was faithful to God. At his core, what God thought about him mattered more than anything else did. At his core, he understood that his life revolved around God.

How about you and me? Are you willing to lay down your life for this gospel? Are you willing to be faithful in a generation that is losing its way? Are you willing to be unpopular? Are you willing to allow God to take your life and shine the light of his glorious presence through it? Are you willing to stand up and be counted? To hear him say, 'I've called you to be a faithful mother, a faithful business-man, a faithful businesswoman, a faithful wife, a faithful husband, a faithful pastor? I don't want you to compromise. I don't want you to give up. I want you to know that I am with you and that I will finish the job, but I am calling you to radical integrity, radical faithfulness, holding out for all that God has for you, by the power of the Holy Spirit, and living for him in a world that will not applaud you.'

Radical purity

by Robin Sydserff

Robin Sydserff is minister of Chalmers Church Edinburgh. One of the church's priorities is training gospel workers through its 'Ministry Associate' and 'Church Leader' training programmes. Robin is Chair of The Bonar Trust, with a vision to train the next generation of leaders for the church in Scotland. Prior to coming to Edinburgh, Robin worked in London as Director of Ministry for The Proclamation Trust. He is married to Sally and they have three children.

Radical Purity: 1 Thessalonians 4:1–12

Over thirty years ago, Jim Packer wrote *A Passion for Holiness*. He wrote out of urgent concern for what he saw as 'the shift of Christian interest away from the pursuit of holiness'.[1] He goes on:

> It haunts me now, as I contemplate the Church's current loss of biblical truth about holiness . . . There was a time when all Christians laid great emphasis on the reality of God's call to holiness and spoke with deep insight about His enabling of us for it.[2]

As we reflect on Packer's words thirty years on, they are deeply challenging.

1 Thessalonians 4 marks a shift in emphasis as to how we are to live as Christians. How we live matters just as

much to God as what we believe. Life and doctrine are inseparable.

Paul's tone is one of encouragement:

> As for other matters, brothers and sisters, we
> instructed you how to live in order to please God,
> *as in fact you are living.* Now we ask you and urge
> you in the Lord Jesus to do this *more and more.*
> (verse 1, emphasis added)

> Now about your love for one another we do not
> need to write to you, for you yourselves have been
> taught by God to love each other. And in fact, *you
> do love* all of God's family throughout Macedonia.
> Yet we urge you, brothers and sisters, to do so *more
> and more.*
> (verses 9–10, emphasis added)

Paul writes to Christians who are already committed to living the Christian life to encourage them to do so more and more. Many of us are already committed to living the Christian life, despite all our struggles and failings. We need to hear the encouragement of God's Word to live this way more and more.

These verses are powerful, practical and pastoral, with great potential for healing and transformation in our lives. Notice, Paul gives us a principle, followed by three practical applications.

Living to please God

The principle is in verses 1 and 2: live in a way that pleases God. Verse 1 says, 'We instructed you how to live in order to please God.' There are all sorts of reasons in the Bible for living the Christian life. It is the best way to live. It blesses others. It shows the world something different and attractive. It reveals the character of Jesus, drawing people to him. All good biblical reasons, but Paul wants to raise our horizons to the summit in saying that we are to live 'in order to please God', to give our heavenly Father pleasure. That is our motivation. As a father, I take great delight when my children want to please their dad. We want to live in a way that pleases God because we are his children. He has done everything for us. He has brought us out of darkness into light, rescued us, adopted us and put the hope of glory in our hearts. And so we want to live in a way that pleases him.

How do we know what living in the way that pleases God looks like? Verse 2: 'For you know what instructions we gave you by the authority of the Lord Jesus.' Paul is referring to the teaching he had given them when he began the church. This instruction had the authority of the Lord Jesus, and the Christians in Thessalonica had accepted Paul's teaching as God's Word. A key verse in this letter is chapter 2:13:

> And we also thank God continually because, when you
> received the word of God, which you heard from us,

you accepted it not as a human word, but as it actually is, the word of God, which is indeed at work in you who believe.

We don't have Paul live in the flesh, but we have his teaching, along with that of the other apostles, in our Bibles. Their teaching has the authority of the Lord Jesus. It is the Word of God. Living to please God means living by the Word of God.

An important question, perhaps *the* most important question today for the church and for Christians is: 'Will we accept the Bible as God's Word, as the supreme rule of faith and life?' If not, then we will be at sea. But if we do, then we will sail a straight course.

Having given us the principle of living in a way that pleases God, Paul then applies it in three areas of life: sexual purity (verses 3–8), Christian unity (verses 9–10) and quiet industry (verses 11–12). Or, to put it another way: live in a way that pleases God in your private life (verses 3–8), your church life (verses 9–10) and your day-to-day working life (verses 11–12). Why these three areas? Well, it is comprehensive, whole-life discipleship: the gospel impacting every area of life.

Living in a way that pleases God – sexual purity (verses 3–8)

The Bible's teaching in this area is clear and consistent. Confusion amongst Christians is not because the Bible is unclear. Confusion arises because of the pressure of the culture and our wariness as Christians in teaching what the Bible has to say in matters of sexuality.

Paul is unashamed and uninhibited in what he says. Never harsh, for he is acutely conscious of his own sin and struggles, and speaks with a pastor's heart, but unashamed and uninhibited. Such clarity and honesty are exactly what the church needs to hear today.

God's will and God's Spirit

Consider first the bookends – how this section from verses 3–8 begins and ends. Without the bookends, the books on the shelf will fall down. Without the bookends in the Christian life, we will fall down.

Verse 3: 'It is God's will that you should be sanctified.' To be sanctified means to be set apart for a holy life like the Lord Jesus. That is God's will for your life as a Christian. God's will is not a wish or an aspiration. God's will is his determined, measured, supernatural, powerful, kind, loving intent for your life. That's one bookend – we've got God behind us, *willing* us to be sanctified.

The other bookend is in verses 7 and 8:

> For God did not call us to be impure, but to live a holy life. Therefore, anyone who rejects this instruction does not reject a human being but God, the very God who gives you his Holy Spirit.

God calls us to live a holy life. The call of God in the life of a Christian is an *effectual* call. It comes with supernatural

power to be who God calls us to be. That supernatural power is the gift of his Holy Spirit, God himself, in
the person of his Holy Spirit, living within you, indwelling
you, enabling you to live a holy life.

God's will and the gift of the Holy Spirit – that is what
is *behind us* and *in us*. It is so important that we grasp this.
Before we consider what sexual purity is for Christians, we
need to be reminded of the power of God within us to
enable us so to live. We cannot do this in our own strength,
but only in the power of the Holy Spirit.

Avoiding sexual immorality

What then is sexual purity for Christians? Verses 3b–5:

> You should avoid sexual immorality . . . each of you should
> learn to control your own body in a way that is holy and
> honourable, not in passionate lust like the pagans, who do
> not know God.

Sexual purity for Christians means avoiding sexual immorality. 'Avoid' is perhaps too weak a translation. 'Abstain' is
better – abstinence, not moderation. Make 'a clean cut'
with sexual immorality is J. B. Philipps' translation.

The Greek word translated 'sexual immorality' is *porneia*
– the meaning of that word would have been clearly understood by Paul's readers. It is a word used consistently
throughout the New Testament to mean the same thing.
Sexual immorality (*porneia*) means any form of sexual
activity outside the bounds of marriage – a lifelong covenant

commitment between a man and a woman. Therefore, sexual purity for the Christian means abstaining from any form of sexual activity outside the bounds of marriage. That is the clear and consistent teaching of the Bible.

So, as Christians, we are to abstain from sex before marriage. But what if I am engaged to, or in love with, that person? What if I am committed to them for life? God's Word says no; wait, there is a better way. Sex is for marriage. Adultery – involvement with someone other than the person to whom you are married – God's Word says it is wrong. Homosexual sex – God's Word says it is wrong. Sexual immorality also includes lust and other forms of sexual sin, such as pornography. It's not just what we do, but what we think about, where our minds go.

If we stand back and look at the Bible as a whole, from Genesis to Revelation, it holds up marriage – lifelong covenant commitment between a man and a woman – as the God-given context for sex. Genesis chapters 1 and 2 are God's account of creation. Genesis 1 is an overview of God's creation. Genesis 2 focuses on the creation of humanity – men and women. The end of God's account of creation focuses on marriage: 'a man leaves his father and mother and is united to his wife, and they become one flesh' (Genesis 2:24). It is striking that God's final word on creation is on marriage and sex within marriage. But then comes the fall (Genesis 3). Sin enters the human heart, and sexual sin is part of that. But in God's purposes to redeem humanity, marriage is affirmed as the God-given context for sex. And it is not just that marriage is affirmed. Marriage is God's picture of the relationship between Christ and his bride, the church. It is a picture of the gospel. What a profound tragedy it is when a church or a nation says, 'God got it wrong.'

As a pastor, I am aware of the pain that is often felt by people who find themselves single and therefore not living in the God-given context for sexual love, that is, marriage. The pain and struggles are real. John Stott, who lived all his life as a single man, writes very helpfully:

> What about us? We too must accept this apostolic teaching, however hard it may seem, as God's good purpose both for us and for society. We shall not become a bundle of frustrations and inhibitions if we embrace God's standard, but only if we rebel against it. Christ's yoke is easy, provided that we submit to it. It is possible for sexual energy to be redirected both into affectionate relationships with friends of both sexes and into the loving service of others. Multitudes of Christian singles, both men and women, can testify to this. Alongside a natural loneliness, accompanied sometimes by acute pain, we can find joyful fulfilment in the self-giving service of God and other people.[3]

John Stott was a well-known Christian, but what he wrote and how he lived I see borne out powerfully in the lives of many people in our church family.

Just a brief comment on verses 4 and 5. As a man, as a pastor, Paul knows the weakness of the flesh, the temptations and the struggles. How do we avoid sexual immorality? 'Each of you should learn to control your own body in a way that is holy and honourable, not in passionate lust like the pagans, who do not know God.' Lust is powerful and dangerous, and leads to sexual immorality. How do we control our bodies in a way that is holy and honourable, and not succumb to passionate lust? The key is at the end of verse 5. Because we 'know God'. Again Paul wants to remind us of the power of God within us to enable us so to live. We can resist temptation because we know God, and his Spirit lives within us. We need to pray, asking God to help us, not simply in the hour of temptation when the crisis comes, but every day.

Protecting others

Living in this way, avoiding sexual immorality, not only pleases God; it protects others. That is what Paul is saying in verse 6: 'In this matter no one should wrong or take advantage of a brother or sister.' Avoiding sexual immorality protects people; it protects us, but more importantly, it protects others. When we engage in sexual sin, it is never without consequence. Sex outside of marriage is to take from another what is not ours to take. Think of the heartbreak and damage caused by adultery, or the effect on a marriage of a secret addiction to pornography. No sinful sex is safe.

Take what God says seriously

This is not casual advice for Christians to take or leave.

We need to take what God says seriously, as individual Christians and as churches:

> The Lord will punish all those who commit such sins,
> as we told you and warned you before. For God did not
> call us to be impure, but to live a holy life. Therefore,
> anyone who rejects this instruction does not reject a
> human being but God, the very God who gives you
> his Holy Spirit.
> (verses 6b–8)

If you ignore this, Paul says, it is not me you are ignoring, but God. This is not Paul's teaching, it is God's. To reject it is to reject God, and that is a very serious thing.

Pastoral implications

The Word of God may have spoken to you deeply and personally. Perhaps there is stuff in your life that you know is wrong, or maybe you are hurt from wrong that has been done to you.

Not a single one of us is exempt from sexual sin. You are not alone in your struggle – you are surrounded by others who struggle. Do not let Satan tempt you to think that sexual sin cannot be forgiven. Do not let Satan hold you in the grip of guilt. If with a repentant heart we confess our sin, it is forgiven – forgiven by the one who calls us to live a holy life and who lifts us up when we fall. Seek that forgiveness now. Put the past behind you and hear God's Word as a call to a life that is good, honourable, full of dignity and worth, a life that pleases God. And live that life in God's strength, God's will and God's Spirit, behind us and in us.

Sally and I have been married for seventeen years. We will soon be getting to significant anniversaries. There were many things that attracted me to Sally. She is an excellent cook and a great encourager. More than anything else, however, it was her purity and godliness that attracted me. And what attracts me to her still is her purity and godliness. The life God calls us to live not only pleases him; it is good, honourable, attractive, and it protects. If you are not yet a Christian, and you have read or heard that the Bible's teaching on sex is out of date, out of touch, I want to ask you to consider whether you really think that is true? Or is the Lord Jesus calling you to a life that is better?

Living in a way that pleases God – Christian unity (verses 9–10)

Sanctification is not just about sexual morality. Sanctification is about the whole of life – whole-life discipleship. In verses 9–10 Paul turns his attention to Christian unity:

> Now about your love for one another we do not need to write to you, for you yourselves have been taught by God to love each other. And in fact, you do love all of God's family throughout Macedonia. Yet we urge you, brothers and sisters, to do so more and more.

The Christian unity Paul is speaking about is not so much unity within their own church fellowship at Thessalonica; rather, it is unity with churches throughout the region of Macedonia. Their relationship with these other churches and believers is to be characterized by servant-hearted brotherly love. They are showing that brotherly love to one another already – there is unity – but Paul is urging them to do so more and more. Why? Presumably because they were facing opposition, persecution, and when pressure comes, there is always a greater risk of disunity. They need to support and encourage one another in brotherly love that together they might be united and strong.

Paul is not speaking about false unity. He is talking about unity between churches and Christians who are committed to, who submit to, the Word of God. He is speaking about the kind of unity that defines a movement like Keswick – a shared commitment to the Word of God.

God's call is for meaningful evangelical unity between gospel churches, genuine gospel partnership around the Word of God. Not partisanship, but partnership. I minister in the city of Edinburgh where there is real, genuine gospel partnership between churches. A number of us ministers arrived at the same time and became close friends. And it is such a blessing to experience that servant-hearted love between Christians, and the practical expressions that flow from it. It is such a blessing to be in an environment where, instead of rivalry, there is a united vision to multiply churches in the city. Love one another, build partnerships, build unity.

Living in a way that pleases God – quiet industry (verses 11–12)

Finally, verses 11–12:

> Make it your ambition to lead a quiet life: you should mind your own business and work with your hands, just as we told you, so that your daily life may win the respect of outsiders and so that you will not be dependent on anybody.

Pleasing God through sexual purity, pleasing God through Christian unity, and then to finish, pleasing God by just getting your head down, leading a quiet life, getting on with your daily life, winning the respect of outsiders – people who are not Christians.

It may have been that some of the Christians in Thessalonica, for the wrong reasons, had given up work and were depending on others. And Paul says, 'No, get your head down and do your daily work. In the normal day-to-day stuff of life, just get on leading a quiet life. Be steady and faithful, and win the respect of people by the way you live as a Christian, ready to share the gospel.'

In a few days 3,000 of us will go back to our homes. Go back with this ambition: that your daily life will win the respect of outsiders, people who are not yet Christians.

Live in a way that pleases God: sexual purity, Christian unity, quiet industry. Live in a way that pleases God: in our private life, church life and day-to-day working life. This is whole-life discipleship. Pastoral, practical, powerful teaching from Paul, with great potential for transformation and healing. But remember, they are not Paul's words. They are God's words, God's authoritative Word to us, about how we should live as Christians in order to please him. It is God's will that we should be sanctified, and he has given us his Holy Spirit to enable us so to live.

Thirty years on, Packer's words have an even greater urgency – the recovery of a passion for holiness in the church.

Notes

1. Jim Packer, *A Passion for Holiness* (Crossway, 1992), preface.
2. Ibid., p. 12.
3. John Stott, *The Message of Thessalonians*, Bible Speaks Today (IVP, 1999), pp. 84–85.

Salvation Means Change

by Patrick Fung

Revd Dr Patrick Fung is the General Director of OMF International. He and his wife, Dr Jennie Fung, previously served as medical missionaries in South Asia for a number of years. As director, Patrick provides spiritual leadership for OMF, which currently has more than 1,400 workers, from over twenty-five countries, serving in East Asia. Patrick was one of the plenary speakers at Urbana 2009 and the Third Lausanne Congress for World Evangelization in 2010. He has two children, Elaine and Samuel.

Salvation Means Change:
1 Peter 1:13 – 2:3

Peter, as one of the early church leaders, was writing to a scattered group of believers. His letter was sent to 'God's elect, exiles, scattered throughout the provinces of Pontus, Galatia, Cappadocia, Asia and Bithynia' (1 Peter 1:1). Now, what are those places if you translate them into today's world? They would be Turkey, Greece, Romania, even Ukraine. Now, I'm asking myself the question: Why is Peter writing to a group of Christians scattered throughout Asia Minor? What is the common uniting factor?

Well, if you read through the whole of 1 Peter, you will notice that in every chapter Peter talks about suffering and persecution. Just now, we prayed for Iran and the believers in the Muslim world. Not unlike our day, Peter acknowledged the common challenge that Christians faced: persecution and suffering. I think the questions that

Christians were asking in those days are very similar to ours: Is it worth it to follow Christ? Is it worth it to suffer in the name of Jesus Christ? Is it worth it to be different?

This passage was relevant, not just in those days, but even today. I could quote many examples. Think of the Syrians – there are 2 million people now scattered across the Middle East, Lebanon and Iraq. They do not have a permanent home. They do not have a permanent identity. Often they live in fear. And the question is: Is it worth it to be followers of Christ?

I'm sure you don't face overt persecution in the UK, but you do face hostility of different kinds. And I realize that even here the word 'Christian' may be strictly scrutinized in the media. Is it worth it? I think it would be easier if we just followed the world, but Peter's encouragement to the believers in those days remains relevant to us.

Right at the very beginning of chapter 1 Peter reminds us that a living hope in Christ makes all the difference to our suffering. He writes, 'He has given us new birth into a living hope through the resurrection of Jesus Christ from the dead, and into an inheritance that can never perish . . . kept in heaven for you' (verses 3–4). Living hope in Christ makes all the difference. It means that even in the midst of suffering there is every reason to be joyful. Verse 8 is very powerful: 'Though you have not seen him, you love him; and even though you do not see him now, you believe in him and are filled with an inexpressible and glorious joy.'

You may ask, 'Really? Is it true? Inexpressible joy in the midst of suffering? Are you joking?' No, I can quote many examples. The one I want to share is the story of Wang Mingdao from China. Wang Mingdao was one of the most well-known evangelists in China. He was a powerful preacher with a ministry throughout China.

Wang was first put in prison in 1955, and he was in and out of prison until 1980. He likened himself to the prophet Jeremiah, who attacked social corruption and false prophets. Now Wang Mingdao was in prison nearly thirty years. When he came out of prison in 1980, the news spread, and many people visited him. Many Western leaders, including Billy Graham, visited him in his little home in Shanghai. Now, Wang Mingdao had this habit when visitors came. He would invite them to join him in worshipping God by singing. But the foreigners were very nervous, because Wang Mingdao sang so loudly that people could hear him at the end of the street. Visitors would be really worried and say, 'Shhhh, aren't you afraid that you will be put back in prison?' Wang Mingdao replied, 'I could sing and worship God while I was in prison. All the more, I can sing and worship God when I am free. I have received the love of Christ. There is nothing to be afraid of; my faith and hope are in him.' Wang Mingdao's joy in the midst of suffering is contagious.

You might say, 'Well, that's a wonderful story, but you really don't know the difficulties I am struggling with. You don't know all the challenges I'm facing in life right now. You are telling me to experience joy. But is it really possible to experience joy in the midst of suffering?'

I want to encourage you. The Bible says that you can experience joy in the midst of suffering. Peter tells us that the key to this lies in intimacy. Let me read verse 8 to you again: 'Though you have not seen him, you love him.' There is a loving relationship. 'Though you don't see him now, you believe in him and are filled with an inexpressible and glorious joy.' Joy is possible in suffering, when there is intimacy. And for Christians it is the intimacy with Christ and intimacy with Christ's followers – community – that brings us joy, even in the midst of adversity.

And let me add just one more point: intimacy precedes imperatives. The imperatives of living for Christ are exceeded by our intimacy with Christ. Without that, God's commands crush us, rather than protect us. Let me give you a personal example. My wife and I served in Pakistan for a number of years. There were many challenges, one of which I can share with you. Our first child was buried in Pakistan. We miscarried, the baby died in the womb and we buried the child in Pakistan. We were devastated. But one of our deepest moments was when a Pakistani brother came to see me and said, 'Dr Patrick, come to my home. I will cry with you, and you will cry with me. But do not cry in front of your wife – you need to comfort her and look after her. God knows your pain.' Now, this brother – I'd only been in Pakistan a year and a half at that time – did not speak Chinese, he was not of my culture or background, and yet when he came to talk to me, I felt that we shared a common bond, a common hope in Christ. Living hope makes all the difference.

Now, of course we know these wonderful truths. So Peter goes on to ask a question: 'How then should we live?'

And he begins by stating something very important as a basic, foundational starting point in verse 13: 'Prepare your mind for action and be self-controlled.'[1] Now that you understand this truth of a living hope in Christ and you experience joy in Christ, prepare your mind for action and be self-controlled.

In an older translation it reads, 'Gird up the loins of your mind.'[2] This was a very suitable metaphor in those days, as many men wore long gowns. Perhaps the equivalent in our world is: roll up your sleeves, or take off your coat. Our mind must be ready for business. For example, imagine an athlete running on the track. Have you ever seen an athlete running in pyjamas? No! In the same way, as Christians who have received salvation and a living hope, our minds must be girded up for action.

Now this concept of 'gird up your loins' was very familiar to the Jews. It is mentioned in the Old Testament. Let me give you just two examples. One is from 1 Kings 18. You remember the story of Elijah fighting against the false prophets? If you read 1 Kings 18:46, it says, 'The power of the LORD came on Elijah and, tucking his cloak into his belt, he ran ahead of Ahab.' The other example is in Exodus 12. It is the story of the Israelites leaving Egypt. They were commanded to eat the Passover, their last meal in Egypt, with their cloak tucked into their belt, sandals on their feet and staff in their hand. They were to be ready, girded up for travel.

Peter says, 'Prepare your mind for action and be self-controlled.' But what action is Peter referring to? The expression 'self-controlled' originally meant 'be sober', 'do not get drunk'. But what Peter is referring to here is not necessarily intoxication by alcohol – although it could be – but more importantly, intoxication by uncontrolled desires. So, Peter says, 'be self-controlled', 'be sober', referring to moral alertness in speech and conduct, having the inner strength to choose and to choose well. Now, of course, being sober or self-controlled doesn't mean joyless gloom. Often I hear our teenagers or young people telling their friends about the Christian faith, and they say, 'Christians can be cool too!' Cool? Yes! Amen!

But here Peter is urging us to be sober, self-controlled and to make good choices, because it is possible to revert to the old way, to make bad choices because of uncontrolled desires. Last week in Latin America, the Pope challenged the church about greed. He said, 'Greed is the dung of the devil' – strong words! Greed is an uncontrolled desire. Another uncontrolled desire is sexual addiction. It is affecting every culture in the world. And it's affecting not just the world, but the church as well! There are many, many other uncontrolled desires. And Peter is reminding us that, with a living hope in Christ, we should not be intoxicated by uncontrolled desires, for we are called to obedience in Jesus Christ.

Of course, the title for today's message is: 'Salvation Means Change'. Change is expected in you. Paul challenged the early Christians in Romans 12:2, 'Do not conform to the pattern of this world, but be transformed by the renewing of your mind.' When our ways of thinking are renewed, our behaviour is transformed as well. God will bring transformation when we really follow Christ.

For the past six or seven years I have been doing Bible studies with a group of teenagers. It's great fun doing Bible study with teenagers. Many of them go to church on and off because their parents go to church. But one thing I noticed about this group is that they swear regularly. You may find it very surprising, but to me it is no surprise, because all the students in the school do that, and so they follow. When I came in to start the group, I didn't make a big fuss about it. But I said, 'In this group there are two rules. One, whatever you say, I'm not going to tell your parents. Two, you can disagree with anyone here; you can express your view, but do it with respect.'

So we continued to do the Bible studies, and about three years later the parents of one of the teenagers called me and said, 'Patrick, I don't know what happened to my daughter. In the past month or so she has suddenly stopped swearing.' And I noticed it wasn't just her; one by one the others in the group had stopped swearing too. So I asked, 'What happened? You were not like that when you first joined the group.' They said, 'Well, all our friends are still doing it in school, but as we came to study the Word of God, we learnt to follow Christ. We lost the urge to do it. We choose not to do it.' That's really remarkable, coming from the mouths of teenagers. That is true freedom! God transformed their lives because salvation means change through the sanctification of the Holy Spirit.

And I am sure you know about the Welsh Revival back in 1904–05. Whole communities were turned upside down. The crime rate dropped, often to nothing, and the police force had nothing to do except supervise the coming and going of people to the chapel. There were no cases for the magistrates to try at court. The alcohol trade was decimated, as people were more interested in what was happening in the chapel than in the pub. Families were changed; renewal happened. You see, when we prepare our minds for action, there is not just the personal effect, but also the social impact. Before I came here, I was praying for the 3,000 people sitting in this tent. You read in Acts 1 – 4 that 3,000 came to the Lord, and they turned the world upside down. Holiness is not just personal holiness; there is a social impact on the community. I can imagine you 3,000 people going back to your world, having an impact and bringing about changes in your communities.

Now if you follow the passage, you will see that Peter gives us three images. The first image is of the Father, the second of a judge, and the last is an image, not of a person, but of imperishable treasure.

Let me begin by talking to you about the image of the Father. 'As obedient children, do not conform to the evil desires you had when you lived in ignorance . . . Since you call on a Father who judges each person's work impartially' (verses 14, 17). Peter encourages the believers: 'Do not conform to the evil desires' – the word 'conform' means 'do not fashion after the trends'. The word translated 'desire' in the NIV means 'impulse' or 'instinct'. Do not just follow your instinct.

I am sure you are familiar with the Freudian concept of the ego and superego. Freud said that human beings are driven by basic instincts, bodily needs, particularly our sexual and aggressive drives. He believed that a physical force motivates us to seek immediate gratification of any impulse, and avoid pain or displeasure. The danger with this theory is that our desire becomes totally undifferentiating, without any boundaries. The modern motto is: Just do it! Just do it! And yet, Peter encourages us in chapter 1:16, 'Be holy, because I am holy.' Imitate the character of the Father in heaven.

Have you read the booklet called 'Cape Town Commitment' from the Third Lausanne Congress? You can download it free. Section 2e is entitled 'Calling the Church of Christ back to Humility, Integrity and Simplicity'. It reads:

> When there is no distinction in conduct between Christians and non-Christians – for example, in the practice of corruption and greed, or sexual promiscuity, or rate of divorce, or relapse to pre-Christian religious practice, or attitudes towards people of other races, or consumerist lifestyles, or social prejudice – then the world is right to wonder if our Christianity makes any difference at all. Our message carries no authenticity to a watching world.[3]

And I would like to add to that, and ask, 'Do we bear any resemblance to the character of our Father in heaven?'

Sadly, often non-Christians look at us and say, 'No, I don't see any resemblance.' And then we become a laughing stock in the world because of the way we live. We are called to imitate our Father in heaven.

The second image is that of a judge. Let us look again at verse 17: 'Since you call on a Father who judges each person's work impartially, live out your time as foreigners here in reverent fear.' Of course, here Peter brings the two identities – the Father and the judge – together as one, to refer to God. Peter is reminding us that we are so privileged to appeal to our Father in heaven. But we need to remember that we are also approaching the Judge in heaven who is impartial. 'Impartial' means without respect of persons, without undue regard to performance or achievements, success or status. Peter is encouraging all believers to live in reverent fear as strangers, passing time as travellers in the world.

Let me just tell you of one example to illustrate the point here. I came from Singapore on a plane just two days ago. When I was on that plane for fifteen hours, the plane was like a temporary home, not my permanent home; I was on a journey. One time I remember when I was on a plane and a soccer team was travelling. They were celebrating because they had just won a match. Some of the team members had had too much celebration, too much alcohol! Things were getting out of control. The steward refused to serve any more alcohol, and so the soccer team yelled and screamed, and one of them somehow managed to punch the steward in the face! When the plane landed, the police came and escorted the whole team away. They did have rights – yes, they had paid for their tickets, for their seats, and they had earned certain rights as passengers – but a certain respect and fear are expected of them as passengers on a plane. There is an ultimate judge, and unfortunately for those soccer players, when they disembarked, their permanent place would not be their homes!

And that's why I think Peter is saying, 'Remember to live in reverent fear of God.' One of the characteristics of the early church is that they were filled with awe (Acts 2:43). Now, you may say, why is Peter emphasizing fear? Isn't it enough to know the love of God? Peter explains in verses 18–19: 'It was not with perishable things such as silver or gold that you were redeemed . . . but with the precious blood of Christ, a lamb without blemish or defect.' Peter appeals to the two most profound emotions of human beings – love and fear. Love captivates us, because we understand that God paid a heavy price for our sins. And yet, fear is important, because fear warns us against treating God's love as cheap grace. What judgment would we merit if we were to trample upon the blood of Christ and treat God's grace with contempt? And that is why Peter urges us: live your life in reverent fear before God.

Finally, we come to the third image – an imperishable treasure. You may say, 'OK, you told us that Peter tells us to live in reverent fear, but how do we do that?' Let me just emphasize one point in chapter 2:2–3: 'Like newborn babies, crave pure spiritual milk, so that by it you may grow up in your salvation, now that you have tasted that the

Lord is good.' Pure spiritual milk – not diluted milk, not contaminated milk, but pure spiritual milk. The Word of God – uncontaminated.

I think Peter is warning us to be very careful about what kind of spiritual milk we are drinking. One example of contaminated or toxic milk is the prosperity gospel. Peter is warning the believers to crave spiritual milk that will lead to healthy growth, not stagnation. Now I must end – my time is up! But I want to leave you with three things. First, take hope – living hope in Christ makes all the difference! Second, choose well – live in reverent fear of God, and do not trample upon the blood of Christ as if it were cheap grace. And third, grow strong in the pure spiritual milk of the living and enduring Word of God.

Notes

1. NIV 1984.
2. KJV.
3. www.lausanne.org/content/ctc/ctcommitment.

Grace to Live Together

by Martin Salter

Martin Salter is married to Sarah and they have three children. He is part of the leadership team at Grace Community Church, Bedford. Martin has been coming to Keswick to work with the youth team for over ten years, and the whole family absolutely love it.

Grace to Live Together: 1 Peter 5:1–14

What are you going to do when the going gets tough? Are you going to press on? Are you going to stand fast? Or are you going to chuck in the towel? In some ways this is the message of Peter's whole letter: 'You must keep going.' Peter has been writing to a church that is persecuted, mocked and ridiculed. A church that is a minority in the Roman Empire. They are worn out, beaten down and on the verge of just chucking in the towel. And Peter has to write to them to say, 'Keep going; stand fast whatever comes.'

Notice how he describes them in chapter 1:1, 'To God's elect, exiles'. In chapter 2:11 he writes, 'Dear friends, I urge you, as foreigners and exiles'. And at the end of our passage, in chapter 5:13, he writes, 'She who is in Babylon . . . sends you her greetings.' Of course, he's not really in Babylon;

Babylon has long since ceased to exist. But he is using Danielic language to say, 'You are exiles, resident aliens – or perhaps better, alienated residents – living in the world, but citizens of heaven. It's tough, and you need to keep going.' And in chapter 5, he winds up his letter with *an encouragement from the eyewitness, to stand fast in grace, aware of Satan's schemes, because you are not alone and God cares for you.* That is our key sentence, and we are going to look at it phrase by phrase.

An encouragement from the eyewitness

So, first this is an encouragement from the eyewitness. Notice what Peter says at the start and finish of the chapter. Chapter 5:1, 'To the elders amongst you, I appeal as a fellow elder and a *witness* of Christ's sufferings who also will share in the glory to be revealed.' And at the end of verse 12 he says, 'With the help of Silas, whom I regard as a faithful brother, I have written to you briefly, encouraging you and *testifying*' – it's the same Greek word – 'that this is the true grace of God.' This is Peter who has seen Jesus' life, death, resurrection and ascension. He has also experienced the outpouring of the Holy Spirit and its transformative power at Pentecost. And Peter is saying, 'Listen to me! Trust me! I've seen it. I've experienced it. You can believe what I've got to tell you!'

A couple of years ago I did something called canyoning in the Lake District. Canyoning is basically making your way down a gorge, mostly on your backside. There are bits that you paddle down and swim through, and there are bits where you have to leap off into a plunge pool and abseil to travel down the gorge. But there's one bit that I really did not like at all. The rock closes right in; it looks like a dead end, but you know it can't be because the water keeps flowing essentially underneath the rock. There's actually a hole in the rock. And what you have to do is hold your breath, go under water, make your way along for a few seconds and pop out on the other side – terrifying, right? So, the instructor explains it and he goes and does it, and after a few seconds you hear him say, 'It's OK – you can come on through!' And you think, 'I'm not going through! I'm going to die. I'm never doing that!' He says, 'You can trust me, I've been through, I'm here.' And sure enough, you take a breath, you go under, reach for a hand, and he grabs your hand and pulls you through. You come out on the other side and realize that everything he told you was true.

That's what Peter is doing here. He's saying, 'Take it from me, an eyewitness to the life, death, resurrection and ascension and the Holy Spirit's power – you can trust me, you can believe me.' And praise God in his wisdom, sovereignty and providence, we have this eyewitness. When everyone else says, 'This is rubbish, this is regressive and unenlightened', you can build your life on Scripture, because it is eyewitness testimony, from people who were there, who have seen it, experienced it, and who tell us it is true.

Stand firm

The second thing we are to do is to stand firm. This is the main emphasis of how Peter wants to close the letter. He tells his readers in verse 9:

> Resist him, standing firm in the faith, because you know that the family of believers throughout the world is undergoing the same kind of sufferings.

And he says the same thing in verse 12:

> I have written to you briefly, encouraging you and testifying that this is the true grace of God. Stand fast in it.

Stand fast in the true grace of God when everything around you buffets you, when colleagues mock you, when mates at school think you're an idiot, when everyone gangs up on you, when you are the only Christian in your family, stand firm. Stand firm in the true grace of God.

I've been reading about a famous minister of old called Charles Simeon. He was born in 1759. His mother was a believer, his father wasn't. They had a lot of money and sent him to Eton. He then went to Cambridge, and during his time as a student he was converted. Actually, he was forced to go to Communion, and when he started to read about it, it changed his heart and he was converted. And when he had finished his studies at Trinity College, the bishop invited him to become the pastor of a church in Cambridge, aged twenty-three. And that's when his problems really began. The congregation didn't want him. They wanted the existing curate, a man called Mr Hammond, and so they blocked Simeon as much as they could. They had an afternoon service, which was in their charge, but they wouldn't let Simeon preach at it. Mr Hammond did it for five years. And when Mr Hammond moved on, they still wouldn't let Simeon do it; they got an outsider in for another seven years. Can you imagine that? Twelve years of pastoring and your people don't even want to hear you preach!

He decided to try to start up an evening service, but the church wardens locked the door and would not let him in. Then the pew owners – in those days you rented or owned a pew – locked the pew doors and wouldn't come to hear Simeon, and neither would they let anyone else use their pews. So, Simeon is there on a Sunday morning with a load of empty pews. At his own expense, he provides chairs. He lays them out in the aisles and in all the little nooks and crannies. But when Simeon was gone, the wardens came and broke the chairs and threw all the pieces in the church yard. This went on for twelve years. A friend asked him, 'Why don't you move on? Why don't you give up?' Simeon responded, 'Because I believe I have been called by God to these people and this place. I believe I have a responsibility to stand fast.' To stand fast in the grace of God.

Yesterday's mission night blew me away. It was incredibly moving to see dozens of people come to the front and make a commitment. But let me say to you, if you didn't come forward and you stayed in your chair, you are every bit as called as the people who stood at the front. It's a different call, but it's no less important, no less valuable. Every person in this room is called somewhere, to some place, to some task, to somebody. And your call matters. You might be the only Christian in your school or your college – you are called there. You might be the only Christian in your work place – you are called there. You might be the only Christian in your family – you are called there. In some ways it is a harder call to stay put, when perhaps the grass looks greener or the new adventure seems more exciting. You have a call to stand fast in a hostile culture. Stand fast in the true grace of God.

Be aware of Satan's schemes

So, we have an encouragement from an eyewitness to stand fast in the grace of God. And we are to be aware of Satan's schemes – that's the third thing. Look down with me at verse 8: 'Be alert and of sober mind. Your enemy the devil prowls around like a roaring lion looking for someone to devour.' The spiritual realm is real. Spiritual warfare is real. And how does Satan attack? You know, I had a little epiphany when I was preparing this. It's an amazing insight – it'll knock your socks off. Here it is: verse 8 follows verses 1 to 7. What do I mean? Verse 8 comes at the end of something. It comes at the end of a load of instructions about something. What is Peter talking about? What is that thing you've got to look out for because Satan's on the prowl? Relationships within the church. Isn't that amazing?

Cancer doesn't shipwreck faith; it often strengthens it. Losing a child doesn't shipwreck faith; it often strengthens it. Marital family breakdown doesn't shipwreck faith; it often strengthens it. What shipwrecks faith? What drags people away from the church faster than anything else is Christians acting like jerks. And so Peter says, think about how you live in relationship with one another. He begins with the elders in verses 1–4:

> To the elders among you, I appeal as a fellow elder and a witness . . . be shepherds of God's flock that is under your care, watching over them – not because you must, but because you are willing, as God wants you to be; not pursuing dishonest gain, but eager to serve; not lording it over those entrusted to you, but being examples to the flock. And when the Chief Shepherd appears, you will receive the crown of glory that will never fade away.

Think about it: this is Peter instructing elders. Do you remember when Peter was reinstated by Jesus after he had denied him three times? Three times Jesus asks, 'Peter, do you love me?' And then what does Jesus say? What is the commission Jesus gives to Peter? He says, 'Feed my sheep.' What's the most important word of those three? 'My' – 'Feed *my* sheep.' It is not your church; it is not your ministry. It is Jesus' ministry, Jesus' church. They're Jesus' sheep – you look after them! Elders, that is your job, that is your role. Do not lord it over them, do not bully them, don't manipulate them, don't take their money from them.

I was talking to Peter Maiden, who's a very wise man, and he said, 'When it comes to leadership, if your identity is in your role, in your position, that is a recipe for abusive leadership.' If all your security, identity, self-worth, value and self-esteem are bound up with the title you hold, that is a recipe for you to abuse people, bully them, shout them down and shut them up. We squash young leaders because they are a threat and might take our job, and our identity is bound up with it. We need to recognize that our identity is in Christ. Our identity is received, not achieved. And so, elders, tend the flock gently.

And in verse 5 Peter moves on and says, 'In the same way, you who are younger, submit yourselves to your elders. All of you, clothe yourselves with humility towards one another.'

Young people, beware of 'angry young man' syndrome. Beware of that kind of zeal that is always critical, always sceptical, always scoffing and always thinking, 'I can do that better.' Beware of that self-seeking and grasping mentality that looks for the role and seeks identity in the power. You've got to be humble and submissive, and in our culture that is hard. Our culture does not value elders and old age; our culture glorifies youth. The Bible turns this on its head. This is a counter-cultural way to witness to the world. Young people, submit, value, cherish and humble your-selves before your elders, because Satan loves it when people puff up, fall out and drop off. Nobody ever gets up one day and says, 'You know what, I'm not going to church any more. I've given up on the faith.' What does happen is that little dissensions break out, relationships break down and people start to think, 'I just can't face that right now. I'm not coming for a week or two.' And before long, they're not coming more than they are coming. And before you know it, people have drifted a million miles out to sea and it's all a bit too late.

One of my favourite films is *The Usual Suspects*. The film is about a gang who committed this amazing crime, led by this arch criminal called Keyser Söze. He's the brains behind the operation, but throughout the film you never see him. He's this mysterious shadowy figure who seems to pull all of the strings. And in the film Kevin Spacey plays this character who is slow of speech and thought and walks with a limp. My favourite part is at the very end. The police have captured some of these criminals and they interview them. And at the end, the final shot, Spacey walks out of the police station, and he drops the stick and stops limping as he walks down the street. The closing line of the voiceover is: 'The greatest trick the devil ever pulled was convincing the world he did not exist.' That's an incredible line for our culture, isn't it? The greatest trick the devil ever pulled was convincing the world that he doesn't exist. Even most Christians don't behave as if Satan is real. We functionally don't believe there is an enemy out there who loves it when we puff up, fall out and drop off. And so we must humble ourselves under God's mighty hand. Humble ourselves – God opposes the proud and shows favour to the humble.

We are not alone

Let's go back to our key sentence: *we have an encouragement from an eyewitness, to stand firm in grace, aware of Satan's schemes, because we are not alone.* We are not alone. We really need to hear that, don't we? We live in Western, twenty-first-century, post-Enlightenment secular culture that says the natural is all there is, that there is no God. We don't believe in God any more than we believe in Santa Claus or the tooth fairy. It is for people with weak psychological make-ups, people who can't cope. No-one really believes in God, and especially not the Christian God – all this stuff about marriage, gender roles and families is so outdated.

And it's easy to catch yourself thinking, 'Am I sure I am on the right side? Am I sure this is right? Have I misunderstood? Perhaps the world is right? Perhaps the culture is right? Can that many people be wrong?' And you need to know that you are not alone. When you feel like you are in the minority, like Peter's audience did, like we do today, you need to know you are not alone. Verse 9 says, 'Resist him, standing firm in the faith, because you know that the family of believers throughout the world is undergoing the same kind of sufferings.'

There is a family of believers around the world. And then in verse 13 Peter adds one more little thing: 'She who is in Babylon, chosen together with you, sends you her greetings, and so does my son Mark.' The churches send their greetings. You are not alone; there is a family of believers.

When you feel as if you are alone, you need to look around you and you need to look back – you need to get a global and historical perspective on Christianity. Yes, throughout the twentieth century 4,300 people were leaving churches in Europe and North America every day. Yet, in that same period, 16,500 people were coming to Christ daily in Africa. That's 6 million people a year coming to know Christ in Africa alone.[1] Operation World[2] have looked at trends from 1900 and projected what the world's population of Christians will look like by 2025. The growth of the church over the last 100 years is explosive. The church which started with twelve now accounts for 2 billion people. You just need to look around the world – to Asia, Africa and Latin America – to realize we are not alone. Yes, our culture is tough. Yes, we are exiles. Yes, we are in the minority, but many people have come to know the grace of God in the Lord Jesus Christ by the power of his Spirit. You are not alone.

God cares for you

We have an encouragement from the eyewitness to stand fast, aware of Satan's schemes, because you are not alone – and God cares for you. God loves you. Look down with me at 1 Peter 5:4–7. In verse 4 there is the promise that 'when the Chief Shepherd appears, you will receive the crown of glory'. We see in verse 5 that God shows favour to the humble. And in verses 6–7 we're told, 'Humble your-selves . . . under God's mighty hand, that he may lift you up . . . Cast all your anxiety on him because he cares for you.' Also verse 10:

> The God of all grace, who called you to his eternal glory in Christ, after you have suffered a little while, will himself restore you and make you strong, firm and steadfast.

God loves you, he knows you, he cares for you far more than you could ever imagine and he is absolutely committed to you. We know this because of the cross. The evidence is the resurrection, and one day we will be with him and enjoy him forever. God was prepared to give his Son because he loves you that much.

So, if tonight you're grieving, stand fast. If you're hurting, stand fast. If you are despairing, stand fast. If you are downcast and downtrodden, stand fast. If you are afraid, stand fast. This is the true grace of God – the encouragement from the eyewitness to stand firm, aware of Satan's schemes, because God absolutely cares for you more than you know or could imagine.

The year is 1812, and Simeon has stuck it out for thirty years at this church. Things seem to have improved, but at the age of fifty-three his health takes a turn for the worse. He loses his voice. It hurts him to preach, and he can only speak in a whisper. But he keeps going for another seven years until he is sixty. Time to retire, right? Well, God miraculously restored and healed Simeon, and he recommitted himself to pastor that church and preach the gospel to the people. He did so for another seventeen years. For fifty-four years he pastored one extremely difficult church because he felt called to stand fast in the grace of God. On the 3rd November that year (1836), he died. Never retired, just graduated.

Let the future glory shape your present story.

Notes

1. Statistics published by Asbury Seminary: http://visual.ly/global-church-shift-christian-landscape.
2. Jason Mandryk, *Operation World* (IVP, 2012): www.operationworld.org.

Vision, Grace, Action
Interview and Call to Mission

Peter Maiden with George Verwer

George Verwer is the Founder and former International Director of Operation Mobilisation, which is a ministry of evangelism, discipleship training and church planting. George and his wife are now involved in Special Projects Ministries (still part of OM) full time. They have three adult children and five grandchildren, and they make their home in England. This is an excerpt from Peter Maiden's interview with George.

It's a great tradition at the Keswick Convention to have a missions night. I've been travelling the world for the last forty-four years, and everywhere I go I meet missionaries who heard the call of God at this convention. A number of missionary societies such as FFM[1] also began at Keswick. George, when you came to Christ, you had an immediate sense that you should be involved in evangelism. Can you tell us more about that?

GV: I think it's because the lady who prayed for me sent me this Gospel of John. I wasn't from a Christian home, but I was a very happy teenager until this woman came into my life and prayed – not only that I would become a Christian, she also prayed that I would become a missionary! And then she sent me this Gospel. I had an interest in the Bible, so I began to read this little book, and I joined the organization that published it, a British mission agency called the Pocket Testament League. So, I got involved in evangelism even before the Billy Graham meeting on 3 March 1955, when I responded to a clear gospel message, which I hadn't understood until then. And really, from the moment of my conversion, I had this passion to give out God's Word everywhere.

How long was it before your concern moved from the neighbourhood, the people immediately around you, to a global concern, and how did that happen?

GV: Again, because I belonged to this Pocket Testament League, I immediately invited one of their great speakers to this very liberal church that I'd become involved with socially. And he gave this challenge and showed films about giving out Gospels all over the world. I was also reading other material about how important the Bible was. And of course, the conviction that the Bible is God's Word is the most important thing in my life.

And this global vision began in Mexico. Tell us a bit about how it spread?

GV: At college I discovered that millions in Mexico had never heard the gospel, not even once. It just hit me – 'I gotta go!' I challenged my roommate to go, and I challenged my mentor Dale Rhoton to go, and the three of us – we were nineteen years of age – headed to Mexico. That completely changed our lives. It became one of the birthplaces of the modern short-term mission movement, and our work of course continues to this day in Mexico and 110 other countries!

And your vision spread to the Muslim world, India and Europe . . .

GV: Well, the original vision was very narrow. I felt that Muslim and communist countries were going to be my main focus. Europe was not yet in my equation. Even India, at that time, wasn't included, because they already had lots of churches, even though millions didn't have the gospel. Places like Iraq, Iran, Turkey and the closed countries – that's where my focus was. Soon after I got married, I went to Spain. Spain was semi-closed, and there I learnt Russian, and that led me to the fiasco in the Soviet Union. I was arrested by the KGB – it was a stupid mistake on my part – and I got thrown out. Then I went for a day of prayer, and that's where the vision for Europe and Operation Mobilisation came. This isn't a normal thing for me, but I had a vision of Germans, Swedes, French, all moving in a revolution of love, reaching everybody in Europe and then spilling over into all the countries, which were part of the original plan.

And so, I transferred to Britain. God had this nation prepared more than any other nation I'd been in, except India, for this message of discipleship, total commitment and world missions. The response was enormous. The first summer we had 200 volunteers. By the next summer, 2,000. And tens of thousands from Great Britain have served in OM, short term and long term, over the years.

And more than fifty years later, George, you must be a very contented man. Is the job done? Does retirement beckon?

GV: No, it's just the opposite. I believe the great problem today is *lukewarmness* among the people of God concerning the lost, both next door and around the globe. I really feel, and I hope it excludes everybody here, that a lot of our Christian faith is just in the head. It's never hit our feet, never transformed our lives, our bank accounts or how we use our time. So, I'm as motivated as ever to preach and to challenge people. Tremendous things have happened, but probably one-third of the world – it used to be two-thirds – have never heard the gospel. And in the midst of all the other things we are doing – humanitarian work, church planting – we must not lose the passion to give everybody in the world the gospel, at least once.

There is plenty of work to do until the Great Commission is fulfilled, but is that work for the British church? So many missionaries now come from the Global South. Is the day of the British missionary history?

GV: You really know how to wind me up, don't you? British missionaries are needed as much as ever before. In places like India where there are now a couple of million believers, of course, our job is to work with nationals. But it's interesting that Indians are saying, 'We still need internationals.' But then, there are other places where there are hardly any nationals. And to me, the biggest mission field for those of us sitting in this tent is Europe itself. In almost every major city in Europe evangelism is going backward. More have not heard about Jesus today than when I spent my first summer in Europe.

We used to talk about the mission fields 'over there'. Is that history?

GV: The mission field is now here as well. Again, don't get caught up in the either/or – it's both! Of course, we've got to emphasize Pakistan, Bangladesh, Mongolia and China – what an open door for China! We hear phenomenal news about huge numbers coming to Christ. It's one of the most encouraging things in the whole world. But we are dealing with 1.4 billion people. The majority of people in China have never heard the gospel, and the way it's going, they never will. So we need this revolution of love and action as much as ever before.

In human terms, OM is a bit of a success story. It started small, and now it's all over the world. Has it been a joy? No trials, tribulations?

GV: Well, I believe in the reality of the Holy Spirit, and even when I am feeling sad – and I've had some very sad news today – I rejoice in the Lord and I claim God's grace. Jesus said, 'If any man come after me, let him deny himself, take up the cross and follow me.' I had a ruthless ego and I had a lot of sexual temptation, but I learnt from Jesus, from the Bible: deny self, take up the cross and follow him. My wife and I have been married fifty-five years, our hearts have been broken many times and we've also had family heartaches. I feel in many ways a very ordinary person with probably more struggles than the average – but we know God's love and that he uses ordinary people. And he uses older people. If you look across the world, many people over seventy – as I am – are accomplishing phenomenal things. I could write a book about it! But I don't have time now.

George, why should people in this tent consider involvement in the mission of God?

GV: Because of God's great love for us! The fact that God loved me and saved me has always been my greatest motivation. Everything I do is a 'thank-you' to Jesus, in much feebleness and weakness. But of course, the need is also there. The Bible talks a lot about the need. I've heard people write that off, 'Oh, you can't go just because there's a need!' We should be careful about writing off things. Life is complicated. The work of God is complicated and huge. The need of suffering people has probably motivated me almost every day of my life.

Which scriptures have been important to you when it comes to mission?

GV: One of the most important things in my life has been memorizing hundreds of scriptures as a baby Christian. Now, often when I am walking, like when I walk between where I stay and the tent, if I'm not talking to somebody, I'm always just quoting Scripture. One of the most significant verses in my life is:

> I beseech you therefore, brethren, by the mercies of
> God, that ye present your bodies a living sacrifice,

holy, acceptable unto God, which is your reasonable service.[2]

And in recent years, with a higher level of struggle in regard to some unanswered prayer and heartbreaks, those last verses in Romans 11 have really helped me:

Who has known the mind of the Lord?
Or who has been his counsellor?

Another favourite is: 'Be steadfast, unmoveable, always abounding in the work of the Lord' (1 Corinthians 15:58).[3] And I believe that, together with prayer and worship, we need radical obedience to the Word of God – even when it's tough. And when we fail – as I have many times – he'll forgive us, pick us up and thrust us back into the action.

For every person who responds and gets involved in world mission, there's got to be a team of people behind them, supporting them. George, what do you say to people for whom that's their ministry?

GV: Well, after living in India for a number of years, which I felt was going to be my life place, the door closed, and I couldn't get a visa. I knew that God was sending me back here permanently to encourage people to get involved in giving and praying. And I started to distribute this book called *Serving as Senders*,[4] because the ministry of sending is just as important as the ministry of going. The Holy

Spirit leads different people in different ways. That's why, especially when we are older, the door may not be open to live in Outer Mongolia or in the middle of India, but with technology we can keep in touch with missionaries. I used to be in touch with forty or fifty people a day by phone and by letters. Now, with email and other methods, I can be in touch with 150 people in one day! And it's so easy to send copies. Remember in the old days, I'd tell my secretaries – it's lucky they didn't assassinate me! – 'Twenty-five carbon copies, please. Twenty-five different addresses.' Now just click, click, click, and twenty-five people get the email. And if you are not into email, I'd really encourage you to get with it. If you are over 110 you are excused, but anybody younger, you need to get into email.

So, you are seventy-plus, George. And you are not slowing down as far as I can see. How do you keep going?

GV: Tea! I learnt in this country how to drink tea! Strong tea with milk. But really, what keeps me going is the Lord and conviction from the Word of God. And I know this will be a surprise word – 'balance'. I remember Dr Schaeffer, walking through a park in London, sharing with me the struggle he had of how much to take in and how much to give out. And I am so indebted to the writings of men and women who have helped me rediscover my humanness, learn to enjoy things and realize God gives us this beautiful scenery – I just love the Lake District – and music and other things that refuel me.

I know there are many of us in this tent who really want to thank God for George. He's been an inspiration to us. We want to thank you, George, for promoting the glory of God through world evangelism and being a tremendous example for us. Please bring God's Word to us now.

GV: In many ways this is the most serious night of the convention, because this is the one night when we are calling you actually to make a specific decision, and that's not easy. We know some people get offended when there is an invitation to call people forward. But I don't believe I would be here if Billy Graham, my spiritual father, had not called people forward in Madison Square Garden. Even when he had finished his message, I thought that I was all right. I prayed because I was a nominal Christian. But as I prayed, somehow I realized, 'I gotta do something!' And I got out of my seat and went forward in front of 20,000 people who believed in Jesus.

Tonight, I would like us to look at Mark's Gospel, chapter one, as we consider this challenge of what I think is OK to call full-time ministry, as long as we define what we are saying. We believe those called into industry, the arts, politics, agriculture or the world of computers – if they love Jesus – are just as much a part of what God is wanting to do. There is a great book, *Your Work Matters to God*.[5] I've distributed many copies. I've also preached on the subject, and many people have told me that they've experienced a whole new wave of joy and fulfilment in their ordinary jobs when they understood the Bible's teaching, when they saw the secular and the sacred coming together.

At the same time, workers are needed who will leave their own culture and go to these other places. And so, we have this one night in which we are emphasizing the need for some people to step out into full-time ministry. Our focus is overseas, but we want to include ministry at home, because many who begin to move overseas, for various reasons such as health issues, end up in full-time ministry here – praise the Lord! And no matter how old you are, you are not left out of this challenge. One of the number one things impacting global missions is the movement of the Holy Spirit among older people, challenging them to serve as 'finishers' or 'second-career' missionaries.

Look at these words from Mark 1:16–20:

> As Jesus walked beside the Sea of Galilee, he saw Simon and his brother Andrew casting a net into the lake, for they were fishermen. 'Come, follow me,' Jesus said, 'and I will send you out to fish for people.' At once they left their nets and followed him.
>
> When he had gone a little farther, he saw James son of Zebedee and his brother John in a boat, preparing their nets. Without delay he called them, and they left their father Zebedee in the boat with the hired men and followed him.

Is the Holy Spirit still doing this today? We say Jesus is the same today, yesterday and for evermore. History shows that people responding to the call of full-time ministry, both at home and overseas, have been a major factor in the evangelization of the world. And let's remember, the last fifty years are the greatest years on this planet when it comes to world missions. Beware of becoming just a small-picture person. Maybe you've got some problems in your church. Maybe you've got problems in your family. Or maybe things aren't going well in your job. All those things are important; it all gets touched on in the ministry here at Keswick. But I think it is also important to be a big-picture person. What's God doing? This is the greatest time in all of history for the growth of the church, for the body of Christ.

Can you imagine, fifty years ago, looking across the world and seeing congregations as big as this convention? You would not see it. Today, brothers and sisters, there are thousands of churches across the world with congregations as big as we have in this great tent. I was in one of those churches a few years ago in India. It was 60,000 strong. All the members had a swipe card to swipe in and out when they went to church!

But here is the other side of the coin I want you to think about tonight. A huge block of countries have been completely left out. And to a large degree we are not seeing that kind of breakthrough in what I believe is the greatest mission field facing those of us living in England: Europe. The door opened for me to go to the former Yugoslavia, where I also got arrested in '61, but very few have gone to these countries. The door opened in Russia, and there was a mad rush for a while. The enemy attacked, and there were some disappointments – the bad news spread quicker than the good news. Today Russia stands as a huge unreached nation that is crying out for help, not just for workers, but for finance and partnership. The need for workers is so great, and we are praying that some of you tonight will go, just as these ordinary fishermen did.

I think one of the biggest things that can help you take this step of faith, regardless of your age, is just that overwhelming realization that God loves you. Let me tell you a story that helps me when I get really down on myself. It's about a family in a thunderstorm. The storm was so bad that even the adults were nervous. Then the parents suddenly realized that their little seven-year-old girl was alone in her bedroom. They ran upstairs, and 'boom!', there was another terrible lightning strike and a loud clap of thunder. They thought that they could see the little girl under the bed, but she was actually looking out of the window. They said, 'Hey, are you OK?' She said, 'I'm fine. I think God is taking my picture!'

My brothers and sisters, God loves you. God wants to use you more. God is concerned about the way you are using your time. The church in Britain needs full-time people in all different ways. This call to full-time Christian service is down-to-earth common sense in the light of the need, in light of the closeness of places like France. How many of you have ever studied French? Raise your hand! What are you doing here? Go to Paris! Think outside of the box! We see non-Christians doing the wildest things; why can't we find more Christians, regardless of their age, taking some steps of faith, taking some risks.

I know that to walk forward at a meeting like this is a bit of a risk. You might be criticized and your emotions might wobble, but God loves you, and he will care for you. We are asking you, would you push the door? Initiative is one of the most key words in the whole Christian message. Too many are sitting back, waiting for something to happen, and meanwhile a third of the world goes into eternity without hearing of Jesus. You can do something about that, and I believe tonight is a night for decision. At least, take that step of faith, and begin to push that door. You may discover that the Lord will open doors to what will be the greatest years of your life. I can tell you that these last thirteen years, where I gave up all leadership within OM, have been just as great as any other period in my life – except maybe those early years after I first came to Jesus.

God bless you.

Notes

1. Fellowship of Faith for the Muslims (www.ffm.org.uk).
2. Romans 12:1 (KJV).
3. KJV.
4. Neal Pirolo, *Serving as Senders – Today*, Twentieth Anniversary Edition (Emmaus Road International, 2012).
5. Doug Sherman and William Hendricks, *Your Work Matters to God* (Navpress, 1987).

Keswick Resources
Enjoy the 2015 Convention!

All of the teaching from Keswick 2015 is available, and here are the various options available to you:

1. Free mp3 downloads of Bible readings, evening celebrations and lectures:

Please go to the Keswick Ministries website and listen or download the mp3s. All you need to do is register, and then all downloads are free of charge. Here's the link: https://keswickministries.org/resources/keswick-talk-downloads.

2. Essential Christian: all teaching – Bible readings, evening celebrations, seminars and lectures – is available in various formats, including CD, DVD, mp3 and also USB stick. These can be purchased from Essential Christian. Please go to: www.essentialchristian.com/keswick.

Other Keswick teaching is also available from this site, and you can browse the Bible teaching catalogue as far back as 1957! You can also browse albums by worship leaders and artists who have performed at Keswick, including Stuart Townend, Keith and Kristen Getty, plus Keswick Live albums and collections of popular DVDs. To order, visit www.essentialchrisitian.com/keswick or call 0845 607 1672.

3. Free online viewing of Bible readings and lectures
Keswick Convention Bible readings and lectures are also available on Clayton TV at www.clayton.tv. Select what you would like to see, and watch the talks online.

Please encourage others to benefit from these Keswick resources.

Thank you!

KESWICK MINISTRIES

Our purpose

Keswick Ministries is committed to the spiritual renewal of God's people for his mission in the world.

God's purpose is to bring his blessing to all the nations of the world. That promise of blessing, which touches every aspect of human life, is ultimately fulfilled through the life, death, resurrection, ascension and future return of Christ. All of the people of God are called to participate in his missionary purposes, wherever he may place them. The central vision of *Keswick Ministries* is to see the people of God equipped, encouraged and refreshed to fulfil that calling, directed and guided by God's Word in the power of his Spirit, for the glory of his Son.

Our priorities

Keswick Ministries seeks to serve the local church through:

- *Hearing God's Word*: the Scriptures are the foundation for the church's life, growth and mission, and *Keswick Ministries* is committed to preach and teach God's Word in a way that is faithful to Scripture and relevant to Christians of all ages and backgrounds.

- *Becoming like God's Son*: from its earliest days the Keswick movement has encouraged Christians to live godly lives in the power of the Spirit, to grow in Christ-likeness and to live under his lordship in every area of life. This is God's will for his people in every culture and generation.
- *Serving God's mission*: the authentic response to God's Word is obedience to his mission, and the inevitable result of Christ-likeness is sacrificial service. *Keswick Ministries* seeks to encourage committed discipleship in family life, work and society, and energetic engagement in the cause of world mission.

Our ministry

Keswick: the event. Every summer the town of Keswick hosts a three-week Convention, which attracts some 15,000 Christians from the UK and around the world. The event provides Bible teaching for all ages, vibrant worship, a sense of unity across generations and denominations, and an inspirational call to serve Christ in the world. It caters for children of all ages and has a strong youth and young adult programme. And it all takes place in the beautiful Lake District – a perfect setting for rest, recreation and refreshment.

Keswick: the movement. For 140 years the work of Keswick has impacted churches worldwide, and today the movement is underway throughout the UK, as well as in many parts of Europe, Asia, North America, Australia,

Africa and the Caribbean. *Keswick Ministries* is committed to strengthen the network in the UK and beyond, through prayer, news, pioneering and cooperative activity.

Keswick resources. *Keswick Ministries* is producing a growing range of books and booklets based on the core foundations of Christian life and mission. It makes Bible teaching available through free access to mp3 downloads, and the sale of DVDs and CDs. It broadcasts online through Clayton TV and annual BBC Radio 4 services. In addition to the summer Convention, Keswick Ministries is hoping to develop other teaching and training events in the coming years.

Our unity

The Keswick movement worldwide has adopted a key Pauline statement to describe its gospel inclusivity: 'for you are all one in Christ Jesus' (Galatians 3:28). *Keswick Ministries* works with evangelicals from a wide variety of church backgrounds, on the understanding that they share a commitment to the essential truths of the Christian faith as set out in our statement of belief.

Our contact details

T: 01768 780075
E: info@keswickministries.org
W: www.keswickministries.org
Mail: Keswick Ministries, Convention Centre, Skiddaw Street, Keswick CA12 4BY, England

Keswick Ministries
HEARING · BECOMING · SERVING

BECOMING LIKE GOD'S SON

God has one main purpose for his people: that we should become like his Son. Christlikeness is something he planned from the beginning and will one day finally complete. But now we are in the process of change, becoming more like Jesus Christ.

Really? How can we overcome the pull of sin? How can we live godly lives in a world like this? Is it possible to change? Keswick 2016 will inspire us with the goal to become like Christ and to live an authentic Christian life that provides a credible witness to the gospel we proclaim.

WEEK 1	**WEEK 2**	**WEEK 3**
16–22 July	23–29 July	30 Jul–5 Aug
–	–	–
Simon	Steve	David
Manchester	Brady	Jackman

FOR MORE INFORMATION SEE
www.keswickministries.org

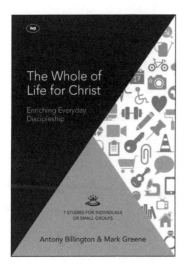

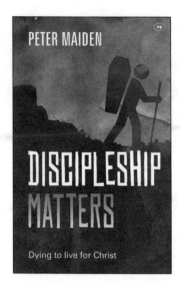

related titles from IVP

Mission Matters

Love says go

Tim Chester

ISBN: 978-1-78359-280-7
176 pages, paperback

The Father delights in his Son. This is the starting point of mission, its very core. The word 'mission' means 'sending'. But for many centuries this was only used to describe what God did, sending his Son and his Spirit into the world. World mission exists because the Father wants people to delight in his Son, and the Son wants people to delight in the Father.

Tim Chester introduces us to a cascade of love: love flowing from the Father to the Son through the Spirit. And that love overflows and, through us, keeps on flowing to our Christian community and beyond, to a needy world. Mission matters. This book is for ordinary individuals willing to step out and be part of the most amazing, exciting venture in the history of the world.

'If you want to fire up your church with a vision for global mission, this is your book! ... It should carry a spiritual health warning.'
David Coffey OBE

'I am sure this book will provoke many to respond to the challenge as they realize that there are still thousands waiting to be introduced to the Saviour.' Helen Roseveare

Available from your local Christian bookshop or **www.ivpbooks.com**